The
Salsa Dancer's
Missing
Manual

The Salsa Dancer's Missing Manual

clave   on2   basic step   timing

Raul Avila

Ankhra Production 2010

The Salsa Dancer's Missing Manual
Raul Avila

Published by Ankhra Productions

www.thesalsaexpert.com

ISBN 978-0-557-39499-9

Printed in the United States of America

Ankhra Productions

Dedicated to all instructors and dancers
who keep this dance alive.

And to all those innovative and creative musicians who inspired this
great music. And especially to Ray Barretto whose music and spirit
has moved me to no end.

To Mirta for being there in the beginning – thank you.

Contents

Introduction   1

Part 1 – Clave   11

Part 2 - The 2 Beat   69

Part 3 - The Basic Step   105

Part 4 - Timing   145

Appendix A   177

Appendix B   183

Appendix C   185

Introduction

...to dance is to live

If the secret is beat upon the drum, the secret will be revealed in the dance...

There are more people dancing salsa today than at any other time in its history. Going back to the 1800s, Afro-Cuban sounds (from where salsa originates), like the *contradanza* and the *cinquillo* rhythm, were already having an influence and appeal internationally. Since then, there have been two major times when Afro-Cuban rhythms have swept this country. The first was in the 1930's with the *rumba* sound, and the second was the mambo craze of the 1950's. Another less dramatic, but significant boom happened in the seventies with a new marketing identity called salsa. Before the name salsa became associated with this music and dance, it was referred to loosely as Latin dance and Latin music. If you wanted to know if someone danced you would ask, "do you Latin?"

More recently, the 1990's kicked off another boom in the revitalization of salsa dancing. Through the impact of salsa congresses and the internet, interest in salsa dancing and music has been unprecedented. More and more people have discovered, or rediscovered, the exhilarating feeling of dancing to this Afro-Cuban based music. Why salsa? A major reason lies at the heart of its musical components – swinging earthy rhythm. Rhythm is the engine of this music, and that is where its universal appeal comes from. Life is rhythm. From our drum-like heartbeat, to the strut in our step, to the ocean waves on a beach, to the sun's rising and setting, all life is a movement of alternating pulses and cycles – rhythm.

1

Salsa music is a modern day version of earthy "bush" music. The drum, with its polyrhythmic sounds, has a unique way of putting us in another mental and emotional state. In fact, in Africa, and throughout many parts of the world, the drum and dancing is a meditative type vehicle for bringing down the spirits of gods and ancestors, and for healing and creating balance in life. The point to all this is that dancing alters our consciousness. In its own way, it helps to heal us and balance us. It lifts us out of our mundane, everyday life. This is what's great about salsa dancing.

This so-called modern living has created a great deal of disconnection with the natural earthly and cosmic cycles and rhythms. The effect of this is that, on some level, we've become imbalanced, out of sync. The end result of an imbalanced state is disease. In a small way, dancing salsa helps to reconnect us back to natural and organic rhythmic sounds. It allows our bodies to move in an inspired way to these rhythms that, in turn, help to align and balance us. Many dancers mention that when they're connected to the music and their partner, they feel a natural high – a true living and enjoyment of the present. Isn't that what makes life so special?

Throughout indigenous societies, dancing was also a way of celebrating life and creating health, balance and connection. In our own way, we can also look at dancing salsa as a way to celebrate life. This might sound over-the-top for some people, but think about it – when do people usually dance? They dance at special occasions, to celebrate a wedding, a birthday, a graduation or some other meaningful event. If you go salsa dancing every week, what are you celebrating? You might say that I just like to dance. This is fine, but the fact that you are dancing is already something special. What is a better way to celebrate that you are alive? What better way to express your spirit? In part, this book is about refocusing your awareness to what dance is really about – to give you another way to think and feel about dancing salsa.

The main part of this book will deal with getting a deeper understanding of the music and basic elements of the dance in order to establish (or refocus) the connection and relationship between the drum (or rhythm, or clave, it's all really the same), and the dancer. This is what is lacking in the salsa world – a clear understanding of the relationship between the dancer and the music.

There is a lot of misinformation going around in the salsa world. Two of the most controversial ones have to do with dancing in clave and the question of which is better; dancing on1 or dancing on2. These topics will be discussed in depth. Suffice to say that many of the arguments surrounding these topics are based more on ego than reality. Once you understand what the music is about, and what the basic step is all about, then you won't be as concerned with what beat you dance on, or whether dancing on 2 is more in clave than dancing on the 1 beat.

But this then begs the question: what does it mean to really connect to the music? Is it dancing on the 2 beat? Is it stepping with the clave? On the most fundamental level, this relationship, or connection, takes place in the heart. It is from there that all movement originates. It is from there that you are in clave. Once you understand this then everything else falls into place. Does that sound too simplistic? It does because it is. What complicates matters is ego - one dancer thinking that his style is better than another dancer's style. In the need to standout and be perceived as "cool" and the best, justifications have to be made. You have to prove why the way "you" dance is better. And this is where all the misinformation comes in.

Dancing salsa is about allowing your spirit to express itself. It's about the "feeling" that lifts you and puts joy in your heart, and a smile on your face. This lack of awareness to the true underlying reason for dancing is what has caused all the rifts in the salsa scene, going back to the 1950's. It's okay to enjoy a particular way of dancing – say on1 or on2. But don't make other forms of dancing inferior to what you like. Unfortunately, this misinformation continues to be perpetuated by both dancers and instructors - who upon closer examination do not really understand the elements that make up their arguments about dancing on 2, clave, or the basic step.

It is from the heart that we connect to the heart of music and dance. In essence, you become one with rhythm. You become the beat. There is no separation between your consciousness and the consciousness of the rhythmic sounds. When you come from this place, it becomes an absurdly insignificant ego trip to get caught up in "on 2 dancers being more in clave," or "on 2 dancing being better than on1 dancing." But, don't get me wrong. I am not putting down dancing on the 2 beat, or the 1 beat. I am simply re-focusing your awareness back to the essence of why you dance, and re-focusing your relationship to the rhythmic sounds of the music. I am also not interested in how "good" someone dances. I realize that there are dancers who have a greater command of their body and look great in the way they move and dance. This will always be there. However, that still doesn't diminish the validity of a mediocre dancer and what they "feel" on the dance floor – whether dancing on the 1 beat, 2 beat, 3 beat, or 4 beat.

Another way that this idea of connection has been diluted is in the way the dance has evolved into this frantic-type dancing where the follower is constantly moving in and out of patterns and spins. Of course, people are dazzled by good dancers who can do countless multiple spins and cool

4

moves. The problem with this is that it can become the focal point of the dance. Cool moves and twenty spins in a row are great, but do it with connection. Let the music move you. It's important that as a dancer you don't use the music as a metronome, but rather as a source of inspiration.

In keeping with the theme of connecting, another important factor revolving around dancing is the social factor. Dancing brings people together. In indigenous societies dancing was an integral way of maintaining cohesion in the community. Usually, when you find salsa dancing, you also find groups of people who are into it as much as you are. There's nothing better than to learn, practice, and spend time with other dancers. Dancing unites people and builds a dance community.

In this first volume, we will look at the various elements that dancers use to connect to this music. It will provide the foundation to understanding the music and dance in order to connect deeper and become a more feeling and expressive dancer.

The names mambo and salsa

In order to understand the terms mambo and salsa, and their relationship to each other, it is important to have correct knowledge of their history and application. The main point is that they are both just "labels" used as a means of identifying a particular Afro-Cuban based music, and by extension, the dance. The label mambo came first. The label salsa came second. Outside of which came first, the word mambo does not have any greater significance to this music and dance than the word salsa does. So-called purists do not like the name salsa, and would rather call it mambo or even Afro-Cuban music. Part of the reason for this is because the use of the word salsa became an umbrella term for Latin musical forms that went beyond the typical "salsa" sound. The term salsa became more diluted in what it represented. Despite this, the majority of knowledgeable dancers and musicians understood that salsa was an Afro-Cuban derived sound that was at one time identified as mambo.

Mambo is an African derived word that came out of Cuba and arbitrarily became attached to this music. By itself, the name mambo had no direct relationship with the music being played. Someone just came along and said, "Hey, play that mambo," and over time it stuck and spread so that everybody identified this type of music and dance as mambo.

The one thing the word mambo identifies more accurately is the "sound" that came out of the 1950's. Meaning, it identifies that particular era of the 50's in the evolution of this Afro-Cuban based music.

The name salsa came out of the New York salsa scene in the 70's. Like the word mambo, this was also another "catchy" label put on the music at a time in its evolution when it needed a new name for marketing and popularizing it. When the name salsa became popular in the 70's, the sound of the music was different than what was being played in the 50's. But, while arrangements and instrumentation may change, the foundation of the music (the rhythm section) remained the same. For this reason, some would still call this music mambo. Keep in mind, while this mambo sound from the 50's is still being played by certain groups today, and there are groups that play more danceable "old school" music, there are also other flavors of salsa, that are not as popular in the NY "mambo" dance scene. For example, for commercial and artistic reasons the music has been watered down and diluted.

The word "mambo"

There is no exact documentation or completely agreed upon version of how this term originated. Obviously, it is of an African origin and through an informal development became associated with a musical form, and by extension the dance. Following are the popular accounts of its origin and usage:

A Congolese word meaning chant.

Also, from the Congo, mambo was a sort of story or lullaby. Children would be sung this lullaby, or "mambo".

Taken as an expression of "How are things?"

Taken as a form of making gossip, like, what's the mambo of the day? Meaning, what's the gossip of the day.

From the name of a type of conga drum called the mambisa.

Name of a voodoo priestess.

As a way of saying "lets swing the music" or "mambear". The word mambo became associated with the last section of the danzon, which was the swinging part of the danzon, and also referred to as the montuno section.

The net effect of this is that the sound is not as appealing to dancers used to the sound of the 50's through the 70's – which is a more rhythmically aggressive sound. An example of this type of music is what is called "salsa romantica." In this style, the singer is highlighted and the rhythm is toned down – which is not what hardcore dancers want.

The sound that came out of the 50's, identified as "mambo" is connected to the sound of the 70's, identified as "salsa," through the intensity of the rhythmic focus and drive of the music. Obviously, the music is different in musical arrangements and instrumentation, but the rhythmic intensity is the same. The music evolved. Innovations and new ideas were explored. That is the nature of musical evolution. Labels obviously represent a particular time frame within this evolution. But the thing to keep in mind is that one label does not make it more authentic than the other. And the fact that one came before another does not make it more authentic.

For convenience and because it is the most popular name today, I will use the term salsa when I refer to this music and dance.

Note: for musical examples used in this book email me at
raul@thesalsaexpert.com.

PART 1

CLAVE

CLAVE

Clave is spirit...the rhythmic power of creation ...
it is nature in simplistic swing... the unity within the diversity...

Clave is a relatively simple rhythmic phrase, and yet it is the heart and soul of salsa rhythms and music. It is the matrix and archetype from which springs forth the logic and structure that is salsa rhythms. Clave is the reason salsa music exists the way it does. It is a primal rhythmic force that generates the infectious swing that inspires bodies to movement.

This is how important clave is: when a song is composed and arranged, the song and the arrangement *must* be "in clave." Everything in the music has to be "in" and "flow" with the clave. To not be "in clave" is to create a disruption in hearing that is sensed as something being out of place, which is described in Spanish as being *cruzado* (crossed or out of balance). To not be in clave is not just being off your timing, it is going against the entire organization of the music.

Over the years, clave's paramount importance has been sermonized by musicians, arrangers, singers, and dancers. The outcome of this has been that clave has taken on a kind of sacred mystique. To invoke the word "clave" is to connect you directly to the soul and essence of this music. You can't get any deeper.

It is interesting that of all the social dances, salsa is the only one that makes reference to a "special" connection to the music that goes beyond just having good timing. Clave became associated with dancing through the idea that, if dancing is an extension of the music, and the music is "in clave," then it follows that the dancer must also be "in clave." But, to hear a dancer say, I dance in clave, is to evoke an air of reverence mixed with ambiguity. It sounds deep, but what does it mean? This question and the definition of what dancing in clave means will be addressed in the *Clave and the Dancer* section.

Note, even if the actual clave is not played, it is always implied. From the beginning of a musical piece to its end, the clave should occur uninterrupted. Once started, the clave will not reverse itself.

Although many dancers associate "clave" specifically with salsa, clave is not unique to salsa rhythms. There are many African and Afro/Cuban rhythms that have a "clave" associated with it. For example, you find clave in 6/8 rhythms, *Mozambique*, *rumba*, and Brazilian rhythms, to name a few. The clave form used in salsa music is referred to as *son clave*. *Son* is a musical genre that developed in the rural hills of eastern Cuba (Oriente). *Son* is the mother of modern salsa (see appendix A for more details).

The Word "Clave"

The word *clave* means "key" or "code" in Spanish, and it relates to that which is essential or fundamental. Applied to African derived rhythms – like salsa, it is a general term that signifies the basic essence of that rhythm.

The word is said to be derived from the Spanish word *clavija*, which refers to a wooden peg.

The word clave can be used in the following ways:
1 - To describe the instrument (two wooden sticks)
2 - To refer to the rhythmic pattern it plays
3 - To refer to the concept and function of the clave

The Instrument - Clave

Clave is traditionally played on two hardwood sticks that create a high-pitched sound. These two sticks are also referred to as male and female. The female stick, which rests (receptive) in the players' palm, is hit with the male stick, being held in the other (active) hand. Originally, these sticks were the same size and width. Over time, there developed another type of clave instrument - where the female stick was wider and had a hollowed out center, which produced greater volume and resonance.

Structure of the Clave

Clave is a five-part rhythmic phrase that takes eight beats to complete.

The following chart shows the clave accents in relation to the beats in the music. An interesting aspect of the clave is that each of its five accents occurs on a unique or separate beat in the music.

	Measure 1 (1st half)								Measure 2 (2nd half)							
8 Beat Phrasing	1	&	2	&	3	&	4	&	5	&	6	&	7	&	8	&
4 Beat Count	1		2		3		4		1		2	&	3		4	
Clave Accents			X		X				X			X			X	

Using the 4 beat count you can see that the clave is played on the following beats: 2, 3, 1, 2 ½(directly between the 2nd and 3rd beat), and 4. In other words, it does not play on the same beat twice.

Clave Origins

While the use of the clashing of two objects to produce a simple rhythmic pattern are found in many cultures, there can be no doubt that the origins of the clave in Afro/Cuban rhythms are found predominantly (if not entirely) in Africa. However, tracing the evolution and development of the clave from its roots in Africa to its use in modern salsa music is vague and difficult. What is known is that this development took place over hundreds of years. During this time diverse African and European musical styles came together and generated new sounds and rhythms.

Researchers have found that certain African traditions have similarities to the clave pattern. Many of these patterns were played predominantly by instruments such as bells. However, it seems that the use of sonorous wooden sticks to play the clave pattern is unique to Cuba.

The concept and use of the clave is one of the most primitive and universal expressions of rhythm (expressed as a binary system).

From the perspective of the African mind; music, drumming, rhythms, dance, and art are a reflection of the universal order, or divine order. And we can see this in the clave. From a numerological and harmonic point of view, the fact that you have two beats against three is significant. In ancient Kemet (incorrectly known as Egypt), the number five was written with two vertical dashes above 3 vertical dashes. The number five comes about from the joining of the male (III) and female(II) – otherwise known as the universal act of creation. This idea of the male corresponding to the number three and the female to the number two is found in other African cultures as well. According to the ancient Chinese, all of life is a manifestation of the number five.

An important factor of this 3-2 model is that it allows us, as dancers, to synchronize to this universal energetic field of rhythm and sound. It allows us to align and harmonize with these universal patterns that exist within us. This is why dancing to music is healing. Listening and dancing to this music creates a natural harmony between our body-mind-spirit and these universal sounds and patterns.

Another interesting correspondence is a vibrating string. When held down at a point that divides the string in a 2:3 ratio, it will produce the interval of the perfect fifth. The perfect fifth is known as the perfect interval of nature. The point to all this is to realize that the clave was originally conceived as a rhythmic device that reflected the order and process of universal patterns of creation.

Historical Development of Clave in Modern Salsa

The clave associated with modern salsa is known as *son* clave. *Son* clave is strongly connected with the clave used in *rumba*. There are many musicians who believe that the clave used today in salsa music evolved out of the *rumba* tradition in Cuba, which in turn, evolved from African rhythmic patterns. *Rumba* is a secular musical form that grew out of the need for recreation and social occasions in an oppressive social and political climate (i.e. slavery). *Rumba* evolved into three main forms: *guaguanco*, *columbia*, and yambu. Of these three, the *guaguanco* is the most popular, and is also the form where the clave can be readily identified as it is played today.

The evolution of the clave from *rumba* continued into the musical form *son*. In *son*, one can clearly hear the clave being performed as we hear it today.

Following is a diagram of the relationship between the *rumba* clave and the *son* clave used in salsa music.

Counts	1	&	2	&	3	&	4	&	5	&	6	&	7	&	8	&
Son Clave			X		X				X		X				X	
Rumba Clave			X		X				X		X					X

In the diagram, you can see that the only difference between *rumba* clave and *son* clave is at the 8 beat (shaded area). The other four accents fall on the same beats.

The Clave Binary System

One of clave's main qualities is that its five beats are broken up into <u>two</u> distinct parts. Each part, or half, takes up 4 beats. One half is made up of 3 rhythmic accents, and the other half is made up of 2 rhythmic accents. Both sides, or halves, of the clave complement and complete each other. There relationship is similar to the relationship between night and day, hot and cold, or yin and yang. The two parts of the clave create a resistance that can be considered as a rhythmic dance. Note, the clave rhythm does not have a beginning or an end. How the clave begins or ends is dependent on the way the salsa song is written and arranged. This means that the clave can begin with either half. The clave can start with the 3-part of the clave (called 3-2 clave) or it can start with the 2-part of the clave (called 2-3 clave).

The 3-2 clave means that within the 8 beat phrasing of the song, the 3-part of the clave plays during the first 4 beats and the 2-part of the clave plays on beats 5 through 8.

The 2-3 clave means that within the 8 beat phrasing, the 2-part of the clave plays during the first 4 beats, and the 3-part of the clave plays on beats 5 through 8.

The following charts illustrate the relationship between the 8-beat phrasing, and the clave accents for both 2-3 clave and 3-2 clave.

2-3 Clave 2 part of clave 3 part of clave

	1st Half								2nd Half							
8 Beat Phrasing	1	&	2	&	3	&	4	&	5	&	6	&	7	&	8	&
Clave			X		X				X			X			X	

3-2 Clave 3 part of clave 2 part of clave

	1st Half								2nd Half							
8 Beat Phrasing	1	&	2	&	3	&	4	&	5	&	6	&	7	&	8	&
Clave	X			X			X				X		X			

As was mentioned, the clave is made up of two parts, or halves, that complement each other. The effect of this two-part structure is to create a call and response, or tension and release quality, which is a common attribute in African rhythms and music. In fact, its binary structure reflects the universal principle of duality. You can think of the two parts of the clave as the yin and yang of salsa rhythms - both sides complement and complete the other. One can't exist without the other. As such, there is not any part of the clave that is more "emphasized" than another. Every accent is as important as the other, and each side exists only in relation to one another.

The full clave pattern, played over eight beats, is considered one unit, or one complete phrase. Note, the basic step also takes eight beats to complete, and is considered one unit.

Another important aspect of this binary structure is the two against three, or three against two, arrangement that invokes a distinct rhythmic relationship. It is said that this relationship is a reflection of natural cosmic forces and structures.

The rhythmic placement of the clave accents is what creates the tension and relationships that define this music's rhythmic identity. It is because of this placement that the music is able to "swing" the way it does. From another perspective, this placement creates a particular rhythmic space between the clave accents that are as much a part of the clave as the actual accents.

Role and Function of the Clave

You can think of this 5-part rhythmic pattern as the blueprint of salsa rhythms and music. And as a "blueprint," it provides the rhythmic basis that organizes, shapes, and governs the Afro/Cuban based rhythms that are the foundation of salsa music.

Clave gives shape to the entire musical expression. It's been noted that clave is the heartbeat of the music, but clave is more than just an internal clock or timekeeper. The placement of the clave accents, and their relationship to each other, give the clave a rhythmic shape (and syncopation) that generates a certain rhythmic tension, which can be defined as a pull or swing. This is the magic ingredient that makes the music so danceable!

Understand that the role of each instrument is to enhance the rhythmic drive in the music – which is to enhance the rhythmic potential of the clave. An example of this is a typical bass line pattern. When the music is at its most swinging (meaning the rhythmic drive intensifies – see appendix C), the bass line will drive the music by playing a rhythmic phrase taken right from the clave. The clave accents that it plays are on the 3-part of the clave – on the and-of-2 (the beat between the 2 and 3 beats) and the 4 beat. See the section: *Clave and the Rhythm Section* for more information on this.

An important point to understand about clave is that it is a rhythmic reference and unifier. In this sense, the idea is not so much to play directly on a clave beat (for the dancer it would be to step on a clave beat), but to integrate layers of rhythmic sounds so that they are all in

23

harmony with each other and fulfill the primary role of intensifying the rhythmic drive. This also means that the space, or beats, between the clave beats are just as important as the actual clave beats. Rhythm is a dance of sounds. How they integrate to enhance each other is what clave is all about.

Clave provides the rhythmic basis that each musician references in order to intensify the total rhythmic experience. It is like flowing with the current, but also having the ability to enhance the current. This is why musicians place a great deal of importance on it. Every musician, percussionist, vocalist, composer, and arranger, is always referencing the clave during every moment of the song, either directly or indirectly.

A good musical arranger is recognized by his/her ability to align the arrangement "in clave." This means that each instrumental section, vocals, and melody are aligned so that they are in harmony with the clave. A singer, for example, to be considered worthy, not only has to have a good voice, but has to have the ability to create improvisational rhythmic phrases that are also in clave. Thus, intuitively or consciously, melodies are created, arrangements are developed, and singing patterns are inspired with the clave pattern always underlying them.

As the polyrhythmic layers build over and interweave with the clave, a sense of being "locked in" to the rhythmic swing and pull of the clave occurs. By building up all the musical components from the clave, the sounds created will complement and enhance and intensify the rhythmic wave that inspires the dancer to the dance floor.

Clave Direction – What makes it 2-3 or 3-2?

To understand clave direction you have to understand musical phrasing. Salsa music is written in 8 beat segments, creating the 8 beat phrasing. This means that the music is constantly cycling through 8 beats. It also means that all the sounds in the music revolve around this phrasing.

Clave direction depends on the 8 beat phrasing, which is established through the musical arrangement. By direction is meant: is the 2-part of the clave playing on beats 1 through 4 in the 8-beat phrasing, or does the 3-part of the clave play in the first 4 beats of the 8-beat phrasing.

If you were to play clave by itself, without any other instrument, you would soon realize that there is no way to know if clave begins at the 2-part of the clave, or on the 3-part of the clave. In fact, you could start the 8-count on the 2-part or the 3-part and both would be right.

By itself, clave is an endless cycle, with no beginning and no end. Each half can take on the quality of being first or second in the pattern, depending on how you want to hear it. What gives clave direction is the musical arrangement, which sets the 8 count phrasing. This 8 count phrasing is made up of the melody line, the progression of harmonic changes, the chorus, and the rest of the instrumentation.

Traditionally, the 3-2 clave was the most common, but since the 60's, the 2-3 clave has become more favored.

When the Count Changes but the Clave Stays the Same

The rule of thumb is that once the clave starts, it keeps playing in the same exact manner till the end. The clave is a constant. Traditionally, the clave never stops and starts again. So even though the music might stop during a break, the clave is still "silently" playing.

There are times in a song when the phrasing changes, thus, changing the direction of the clave – even though the clave continues playing the same way. This means that the emphasis of the 1 beat shifts one measure so that what was the 5 beat (in the 8 beat phrase) becomes the 1 beat. This usually happens when there is a break in the music, but can also happen in the continuous flow of the music.

Using the example of a break in the music, one way this change can happen is when the music stops during the first 4 beats of the 8 beat phrasing, and then it will come back in on the very next measure – which would have been the 4 through 8 beats. But when it comes back in, it comes back in as the 1 beat, resetting the 8 beat phrasing. In this case, because of the phrasing change, the clave direction also changes. Remember, **if the phrasing changes, the clave direction changes.**

In the chart below, notice in the 8 beat phrasing row, that in measures 3 and 4, the counts are both 1234. In measure 4, the shaded box shows 1234, breaking the 8 beat pattern - which would have continued as 5678. This happens because of a shift in the arrangement of the music that realigns where the 1 beat begins. A common place in a song that it happens is at the transition between the introduction of the song - where the singer sings on his own - and the *montuno* or swing part of the song (where the chorus comes in and the singer improvises). It is also common in the transition from the *montuno* section to the bridge. Notice also, that the clave pattern does not change.

	1	2	3	4	5	6	7
4 count	1234	1234	1234	1234	1234	1234	1234
8 beat phrasing	1234	5678	1234	1234	5678	1234	5678
clave	XX	X X X	XX	X X X	XX	X X X	XX

As you can see, in the first measure, the clave is in 2-3 because the 2-part of the clave is playing with the 1234 beats, and the 3-part of the clave is playing with the 5678 beats. But, in measure 4, the music shifts and starts the 1 beat where the 5678 beats would have been. This now shifts the direction of the clave. The 3-part of the clave is now playing with the 1234 beats, and the 2-part of the clave is playing with the 5678 beats – making the clave direction 3-2.

There are on2 purists (usually leaders), who when they hear this change, will stop their dance and realign their basic step so that they're going back on the realigned 1 beat and forward on the 6 beat again. This brings up a controversial topic. Is it necessary for the man (leader) to always go forward on the count 6, and go back on count 2 in the on2 style? Is there anything inherent in the music that dictates that? The answer is no. The on2 standard for the leader going forward on 6 and back on 2 is totally arbitrary. This means that if the leader wanted to go forward on 2 and back on 6 it would be just as fine. What has happened is that the idea of going forward on 6 and back on 2 went from being a "way" of dancing, to the only way to dance (for on2 dancers). In other words, it became dogma. It has become so ingrained in the minds of dancers that when they see a guy dancing 2 forward and 6 back, they look down on him with the attitude that he doesn't have his timing together – he's flip-flopped. From the perspective of the music, the music doesn't care where you begin your dance.

The only valid reason dancers give for the leader going back on 2 and forward on 6 is that going back on 2 is a courtesy to the woman when starting the dance. That is not a valid reason. It's chivalrous but has no "real" validity when it comes to "where" you dance in the music. A true leader can start a woman
forward or back on any beat.

Musical Example of a Change in the Phrasing

We will take the song, Sujetate *La Lengua* by Eddie Palmieiri. The clave is played throughout so you can hear how the direction of the clave changes because of the phrasing change.

The song begins in 2-3 clave.
At 0:11 – the phrasing changes and the clave direction is now
3-2.
At 1:17 - the *montuno* section comes in and the phrasing changes making the clave direction 2- 3 again. It will stay 2-3 clave for the rest of the song.

Notice how the clave remained the same throughout. It was the musical arrangement (the 8 beat phrasing) that shifted where the 1 beat begins, thus shifting the clave direction.

Clave and 4/4 Timing

The clave pattern is played over a 4/4 time signature. Some musicians will more correctly state that it is really 2/4 time. However, 4/4 has become the standard. The result is the interaction of two pulses occurring simultaneously, which complement each other. Again, we come back to this binary concept. Except now, it is the straight beats of 4/4 against the syncopation of the clave accents. Because 4/4 is the underlying "base" over which clave is layered, it can be said that 4/4 is in "clave" with clave.

Counts	1	&	2	&	3	&	4	&	5	&	6	&	7	&	8	&
Clave			X		X				X			X			X	

The chart above shows the clave accents (in 2-3 clave) in relationship to the 8 beat count. Notice that two of the clave accents are on downbeats (the 3 and 5 beats), and three of the clave beats are on the upbeats, or syncopated beats (the 2, & of 6 and 8 beat).

The pulse of clave and the pulse of 4/4 are dependent on each other and complement each other. So, in the same way that the two halves of the clave complement and complete each other, so it is with the clave and 4/4 relationship. Another way of understanding this is: clave lives in 4/4 and 4/4 lives in clave.

It is because of this rhythmic relationship that all four beats in the music are in clave with clave. The space between the clave beats are also in clave, and are just as important. This is a point that is lost on many dancers in their understanding of clave. Many people tend to think that the clave beats are the only vital parts to pay attention to, but the space between the clave accents are just as vital. You can hear this by listening to the clave being played with the conga

29

rhythm. You can here how the space between clave accents can be emphasized to create a harmonious interplay between the conga accents and clave accents. With this understanding we can begin to see how dancing on1 is just as "in clave" as dancing on2.

What does it mean to have a Clave Sense?

Having a clave sense means having a "salsa music" sense. It means that you have been listening to this music and have a "sense" for the logic and dynamic of the music. This logic refers to the general structure of a salsa song as well as the common rhythmic patterns that define the salsa sound – the bass line, conga drum, the *coro*, the piano line, common riffs and breaks in the music. This also implies that you don't have to have any knowledge or understanding of music to have a clave sense.

Having a clave sense does not mean that you have to know where the clave is playing in the music, although that can be a part of it. To understand this is to realize that the music is an extension of the clave. So if you can "sense" what the music is doing, and be able to flow with that, either as a musician, or a dancer, then you have a clave sense. There are two approaches to having a clave sense. One is based on intuition and feeling, the other is based on knowing the musical structure of clave and understanding how it fits with the musical components. Both ways work and are valid.

Having this "sense" for the music is a way of connecting deeper to it. On the most basic level, it is what you "feel" when you hear this music that compels you to get up and dance. Taking this further, when you are familiar with the dynamics of the music, in other words, have a "clave sense," it then sets the stage for greater creativity and expression.

For dancers, having a clave sense relates to body movements and gestures and steps and how they are done with the music. Many dancers acquire the flavor of moving with the music in certain ways by watching other dancers, as well as through their own natural means of expression.

How to Develop a Clave Sense

For dancers, there are two components in developing a clave sense. The first is being able to hear and sense the patterns in the music, and the second is to translate the experience of those musical patterns into steps and movement. Having a clave sense is the same as having a musicality sense.

A key to working with the music is to remember that every sound in the music is revolving around the 8 beat phrasing. The next key is that you have to listen to enough of this music so that you become familiar with the "tendencies" of the music, and the general patterns of the music. Most dancers develop this sense after years of listening, as well as dancing. So, you definitely have to put the time into just listening.

When I say listening, I mean *really* listening. Take a song you really enjoy and consciously listen to what it is doing. Listen to the overall rhythmic phrasing. How does it move from one section to another? Where does the song pick up? Where do you hear the stronger accents in the music? Where do the breaks in the music occur? How do the breaks take place rhythmically? Pick out the strong recurring accents that you can hear very well. Maybe it's the piano line, or the cowbell. How does it relate to the general phrasing of the music? How does it relate to your basic step?

After you've gone through one song, go through at least two others, and do the same thing. Make sure that you listen to songs that are of the same type of salsa or "sound." For example, die-hard New York dancers prefer to listen to the rhythmically aggressive sounds of the 60's and 70's, before the music became diluted and commercialized. Here are three popular songs from that era that give a good sense of the dynamics of that type of music.

1. Bilongo – Eddie Palmieri
2. Indestructible – Ray Barretto
3. Te Conozco – Willie Colon

Exercises to develop a clave sense

Here are two exercises you can work with to begin to move and experience your dance more connected to the music – which goes with developing a clave sense. First, make sure that you have a good handle on the dynamics of the song you've been listening to. Then, take that song and establish your basic step to it. You may need to count to start your basic correctly. But after your basic is going, begin to hear just the music so that your basic step becomes anchored to what you're hearing, and not your counting. You may want to close your eyes so you can focus more on the sounds. The idea is to integrate your hearing and your basic step so that you can experience the interplay between them. You become so familiar with where your basic step should be in relation to the rhythm that you don't have to rely on counting to maintain your timing. Eventually, you want to release the counting totally, while maintaining your basic step timing perfectly. This takes some time to really develop, but it will make you a much better "feeling" dancer.

Here's another simple exercise you can do to begin to develop the feeling of creating an improvised movement to go with the music. Establish your basic step with the music, and when you get to certain breaks and crescendos in the music, perform a movement that expresses that place in the music. You can work out a movement ahead of time or you can be spontaneous. The point is to really match a movement to the music. It could be tapping your foot along with a break. Or it could be shoulder shimmies during a timbale solo. Whatever! The point is to reach that place, express yourself, and then come back in to your basic perfectly.

As an approach to this exercise you can also get into the habit of watching the way dancers with nice movement and musicality dance to the music. Then try to emulate that in your own dance. The idea is not to become a clone but to experience, in your own way, the movement you like. Eventually, you make that movement your own, and it can become a springboard for exploring other movements and means of expression.

Another good practice is to clap out the clave when listening to a song. By doing this you will see how the clave integrates itself with breaks and certain dynamics in the music. Again, it will deepen your understanding of the music as well as your "feeling" of the music. In fact, another great exercise is to clap the clave while you do the basic step. This is similar, though more challenging, to doing your basic step with the conga drum. At first you can depend on counting to sync your steps and the clave and then you can just go with the feeling of it, dropping out the counting.

Learning to play a percussion instrument is also very helpful. The basic conga rhythm is a great way to get started. You can even go out and buy a pair of inexpensive clave sticks to play along with. The more you immerse yourself in these rhythms the better "feeling" dancer you will become. It takes time but it will be well worth it.

Example of Working with a Song to Develop a Clave Sense

This exercise will help to develop the recognition of patterns and tendencies in a typical "classic" salsa song. I will use one of my favorite Ray Barretto tunes entitled *Oye La Noticia*. Recorded in 1972, it represents the rhythmically aggressive urban sound coming out of New York in the 70's. This is part of that "classic" New York sound that many serious dancers prefer dancing to today.

Within the first 7 seconds you can hear the strong conga rhythm playing underneath the trumpets.

00:09 That leads to a break and then...

00:12 A timbale roll to bring the band back in on the count of 1. The piano line is pronounced when the music comes back in.

Again, notice the strong rhythm section, especially the conga rhythm, as it drives the music forward.

00:16 At this point there is hit by the timbale as a lead-in to the singing section. While this is an incidental sound in the general song, it highlights the importance of accenting on the 8th beat of the 8 count phrasing, which also correlates to the accent on the 8 beat of the 2-3 clave. This is also a hint (or clave sense) that a dancer can hit that same accent through some body movement or footwork, thus, developing a clave sense through the dance.

The song continues with singing and trumpet accompaniment. Underneath this, the rhythm section is maintaining its aggressive drive.

00:50 At this point a break occurs that leads to the trumpets playing the melody of the *coro* (or chorus) that will be coming up. Only the piano and bass play with the trumpets. This is an arrangement technique that really excites listeners and dancers – building up the anticipation as the song moves into the swinging part of the music. Usually, the band drops out and one instrument plays a rhythmically tasty phrase for a few bars before the rest of the band comes in. A more common example of this is the use of just a piano riff.

00:56 Just before the music comes back in, the rhythm section plays a break that is exactly the rhythm of the 3-part of the clave. This is one of the most important break patterns in salsa music – especially in the more rhythmically aggressive "classic" style. It aligns with the clave and creates a potent rhythmic transition that propels the music forward. Again, the more expressive and knowledgeable dancers will do a movement or styling to go with this break.

The music is now in the "swinging" part of the song, where the *coro* and improvisations by the lead singer begin. Notice the bass line pattern. Also, a bell pattern can be heard - driving the rhythm forward.

1:46 The piano solo starts. What I want you to notice at this point is the heavy emphasis the rhythm section plays on the 8 beat – a strong sounding duum! Again, accenting the 8 beat of the 2-3 clave. It provides a strong rhythmic transition to the piano solo. You can hear this same type of emphasis on other recordings when a piano or tres solo is coming up.

During the piano solo you can here various accents and interplay by the rhythm section and the piano. At 1:58 the timbale begins a riff that the piano plays along with. Very tasty and inspiring. A dancer can definitely create a movement to match that.

As the piano continues soloing the timbale is placing a few accents at rhythmically potent spots. You can take those accents and incorporate them into your body movement. When you really look at it, as a dancer you are another rhythmic instrument. So doing accents through footwork or body movement that coincide with a conga riff or timbale riff builds your clave sense or sense of the music.

2:54 Another break occurs leading into the conga solo.

During the conga solo you can hear the piano line clearly, as well as the bell patterns.

3:50 The trumpets come in, and a trumpet solos while the other two trumpets play a riff behind the soloist. The music is at the height of its rhythmic intensity.

The coro and singer come back in and then at -

4:17 Listen to the timbale riff while the singer is improvising. It iis riffs like these, along with the intense rhythmic drive, that make this music so much more powerful for dancers than other types of salsa sounds.

Around 4:36 the trumpets begin to come back in again, building into one more crescendo before the end. This time the singer and coro continue while the trumpets blare into rhythmic harmony.

Clave and the Rhythm Section

We now take a look at how the clave participates in the rhythmic structure of the instruments in the rhythm section. The typical instruments that make up the rhythm section are: conga, bongos/cowbell, timbales, piano, and bass. You can also include the guiro, maracas, and tres as well.

The rhythm section can be broken up into two rhythmic categories: those instruments that play one-bar phrases, or 4 beats long and then repeats; and those that play two-bar phrases, or 8 beats long and then repeats.

As the clave is a two-bar rhythmic phrase, it aligns more naturally with the instruments that play two bar phrases. However, both one-bar and two-bar phrases harmonize equally with the clave.

One Bar Phrases - 4 Beats

The instruments that play one bar phrases are the conga, bongos, cowbell, guiro, and bass. What is interesting is that the conga, cowbell and guiro play the same rhythmic pattern: a one against two pattern. The following chart illustrates the rhythmic accents for each of these instruments over two bars of music (8 beats).

Counts or Beats	1	2	3	4	5	6	7	8
Conga		X		XX		X		XX
Cowbell	X	XX	X	XX	X	XX	X	XX
Guiro	X	XX	X	XX	X	XX	X	XX

Notice in the chart above that the one against two rhythmic pattern of the conga takes 4 beats to complete. For the cowbell and guiro, the pattern (the one against the two)

38

takes place within 2 beats – so that it plays that rhythmic pattern twice within 4 beats.

The function of these one bar patterns is to establish a consistent and vital groove - in other words, to establish the rhythmic drive of the music, to push the music. The conga rhythm is similar to drums in swing music - it accents the back beats, or the 2 and 4 beats. In fact, the conga becomes the most consistent sound in the rhythm section. This is why beginners who want to learn to dance on the 2 beat can reference the conga drum with 100% accuracy. Also, the open sound of the conga on the fourth beat complements the clave well and creates a shift in the rhythmic stress. This gives extra emphasis on the fourth beat of the measure – a common African attribute. The net effect is to weaken the accent of the strong downbeat on one. This sound on the fourth beat creates a rhythmic interval with the clave that drives and swings the music. This four beat, at the 3-part of the clave, is referred to by musicians as "ponche." This is that beat in the clave that was emphasized in the tune "Oye La Noticia," in the previous section on working with a song to develop a clave sense.

Although all the instruments that play one bar patterns can play it straight (i.e. the same way) for every measure, like the chart above, they also have the flexibility to modify their rhythmic pattern to align with the direction of the clave. This means that they create an 8 beat phrase, while still maintaining the rhythmic drive you get with every 4 beats. The way this is usually done is by dropping out one accent on the 2-side of the clave.

For example, in the chart below there are two variations that the cowbell pattern can play. In the first pattern, labeled as "straight," the cowbell plays the same rhythmic figure throughout – every 4 beats. In the second pattern, labeled "w/clave," the cowbell plays the 2-part of the clave the same way the clave does. On beats 6 and 7, you can see that both the cowbell and clave are synchronized. In the row labeled "straight," the cowbell plays that extra accent between beats 6 and 7. In the row "cowbell w/clave" the accent drops out on the "&" of 6 (shaded box).

4 Count	1	&	2	&	3	&	4	&	1	&	2	&	3	&	4	&
8 Count	1	&	2	&	3	&	4	&	5	&	6	&	7	&	8	&
Cowbell - solo	X		X	X	X		X	X	X		X	X	X		X	X
Cowbell - with clave)	X		X	X	X		X	X	X		X		X		X	X
Clave	X			X			X				X		X			

40

The Bass Line as a One Bar Rhythmic Pattern

Another common one-bar phrase is played by the bass line. The bass line gives us another perspective on the influence of the clave in creating a powerful rhythmic drive.

The bass pattern that most concerns us is the rhythmic pattern that is played when the *montuno* or vamp section of the tune is played. This is the part of the music that "swings".

The following diagram highlights the part of the clave that the bass line will play.

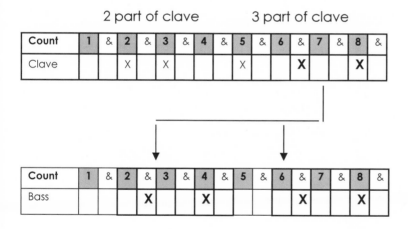

Count	1	&	2	&	3	&	4	&	5	&	6	&	7	&	8	&
Clave			X		X				X		**X**				**X**	

Count	1	&	2	&	3	&	4	&	5	&	6	&	7	&	8	&
Bass			**X**				**X**				**X**				**X**	

This bass pattern is taken right out of the last two accents of the three part of the clave. This is a perfect example of how a part of the clave rhythm can be "lifted out" and be used to intensify the "swing" of the music.

It is the dynamic relationship of these two clave accents that provide the necessary syncopation and rhythmic movement that makes this music so infectiously danceable.

41

Two Bar Phrases - 8 Beats

Those instruments that typically play two bar phrases are the piano, tres, timbale cascara rhythm, and some bell patterns.

The following table shows the accents of the cascara rhythm and a typical piano line rhythm. Notice how the last three beats (beats 6, 7, and 8) are almost the same between the cascara and piano. The clave is also given to show how the two rhythms interweave with it. As was mentioned in a previous section, the clave is a facilitating rhythmic device that seeks to unite various rhythmic lines so that they can harmonize with each other. This is clave's important feature. It's not about creating a rhythmic line that plays the same accents as the clave. It's about rhythmic lines that complement and harmonize with the foundational rhythm of clave. This means in creating a musical arrangement, a musician will seek the best sounding melodies and rhythms and phrases that will work together – that will harmonize together – that will be in clave. **From this point we can extrapolate, as dancers, that being with the clave is not about what beat you step on, but how you integrate your dance fully to the entire musical sound and not just specific clave beats.**

Counts	1	&	2	&	3	&	4	&	5	&	6	&	7	&	8	&
Cascara	X		X		X	X		X	X		X	X		X		X
Piano	X		X	X		X		X		X		X		X		X
Clave			X		X				X		X		X			

The cascara rhythm is a very common rhythm played on the side of the metal timbale drums. It is typically played during the introduction of a song, the ending, and solos. Dancers can acquire a great sense of the 8-

beat phrasing by learning to recognize the cascara rhythm and dancing to it.

The piano line is similar to the cascara rhythm, but with the addition of melody and harmony – which allows you to hear the 8-beat phrasing more distinctly. Note, this type of piano line is usually played during the "swing" part of the song, also known as the *montuno* section.

From the role that both one bar and two bar phrases play, you can see that the clave is inextricably connected to the 4/4 time structure. Each type of phrasing is serving the purpose of creating a consistent rhythmic groove that translates into something we have a natural tendency to move to.

CLAVE and the DANCER

"I hate when people talk about dancing on two...when this dance came out there was no such thing as dancing on two. You danced on clave, period. People took this and bottled it, systematized it . What do you mean dancing on two? I'm dancing on clave."

- Luis Maquina Flores

Many dancers have heard the expression "dancing on clave," or "dancing in clave." However, if you ask the average dancer what that means, the "knowledgeable" ones will say that it means dancing on2. This is the most popular definition for dancing in clave. There are other views, such as: it's feeling the music; or taking steps that go with the clave beats; or moving your body a certain way to the music.

This idea of dancing "in clave" originated during the mambo craze of the 1950's. It should be noted that the idea of dancing in clave came out of Cuba and that it was already a way of connecting to the music, especially *Rumba*. But it wasn't until the heyday of mambo in the 50's that this idea became firmly established in New York.

Though there is no way to verify it, there can be little doubt that it was the musicians that put the idea of dancing "in clave" into the heads of dancers. Pedro Aguilar (Cuban Pete), who was a popular dancer in New York during the 50's, tells the story about how he learned to dance "on clave." He says that Machito (the famous singer of the Machito Orchestra) came up to him at a dance and said, "I like the way you dance, but you're not on clave." The story goes that Machito then went on to explain the subtleness of the clave, and the difference between dancing on one, and dancing on two.

Since the 1950's, this idea of 'dancing on2 equals dancing in clave has been passed along informally among dancers. But, it's only been since the early 90's, with the increased interest in salsa dancing and music (especially through the internet and salsa congresses), and the popularity of on2 dancing, that this idea has developed into a belief bordering on dogma. With this revitalization of salsa, a new generation of dancers hungered for knowledge concerning this music and dance. They wanted to know about the mysterious clave. They wanted to know about this on2 thing. To fill this knowledge gap, a new wave of teachers, dancers and on2 websites took it upon themselves to break down just *how* the on2/clave connection actually works. In other words, they wanted to "prove" the idea that dancing in clave "really means" dancing on2. Unfortunately, all the arguments supporting this claim are flawed. These arguments will be closely examined later in this section.

This chapter will provide information and insights into the relationship between the dance and clave, and if this on2/clave connection has any real substance behind it.

Clave and the Basic Step

Any reference to the basic step refers to any style of basic step where you have 3 steps over 4 beats for the forward half and 3 steps over 4 beats for the back half. It doesn't matter what beat you dance on.

Clave and the basic step developed separately and for different reasons. Clave came out of the Afro-Cuban rhythms that are the foundation of salsa music. The basic step came out of a need to partner dance in a logical and symmetrical arrangement.

Clave is a rhythmic pattern that is completed over 8 beats. It is a unique rhythmic statement that, while made up of two parts, has to be taken as a complete phrase.

The basic step is also completed over 8 beats, but that's where the similarities with the clave end. Clave is a rhythmic pattern where the relationship between each of its accents produces its distinct sound. Each of the clave beats is played at a different point in the music. Meaning, it does not duplicate itself and its structure is asymmetrical. Over the two measures, or 8 beats, the clave does not play the same beat twice, nor the same rhythmic pattern.

The basic step is symmetrical. It was developed to hook into the underlying regularity of 4/4 timing. Clave was never a factor in its creation and usage. The main consideration in its development was: can I keep time with the music, and, can I create a step pattern where I can mirror, in a symmetrical and balanced manner, my partners steps – so that we can create a logic and structure for dancing with each other. Because of these constraints the basic step has to duplicate the beats it steps on so that the forward half of the basic are on the same beats as the back half of the basic.

Once you understand the role of these two elements, you can then understand their relationship to each other and the music.

Clave is integrated with the 4/4 timing of the music, as well as all the sounds in the music. The basic step is not integrated with the clave directly. Its sole purpose is to hook into the 4 beats per measure of the music – which is the underlying time basis of the clave. The basic step indirectly connects with clave through the 4/4 timing.

Four Popular Arguments Explaining Why On2 Dancing Equals Dancing in Clave

Based on the understanding of clave and the basic step that has been set down in this chapter, we will now examine and evaluate the validity of the four strongest arguments used to explain why dancing on2 is dancing in clave. In order to check the validity of these reasons we will establish a set of criteria. The following three points, which I will call "clave rules," will be the basic criteria used to test the validity of these arguments.

Rule 1 – Recognize that the clave is an integrated whole that is greater than the sum of its parts.

Rule 2 - The basic step was developed to align the dancer to the 4/4 timing of the music - not clave.

Rule 3 - Arranged and composed correctly, every sound in a salsa song is in clave.

The Arguments

#1

The following are two quotes supposedly from Cuban Pete, one of the mambo legends of the Palladium era of the 50s:

*Dancing on the 1 beat is dancing **to** the music, dancing on the 2 beat is dancing **in** the music.*

*Dancing on the 1 beat is dancing **to** the melody, dancing on the 2 beat is dancing **in** the rhythm.*

Essentially, these two lines are saying the same thing: that dancing on the 1 beat is a superficial way to connect to the music (**to** the music implies *outside* the music) and that dancing on the 2 beat connects you deeper (**in** the music) to the core and essence of the music – thus, clave.

These quotes go right to the heart of the controversy that pitch on1 dancing against on2 dancing. On2 dancers tend to consider their way of dancing superior to other forms of dancing salsa (such as dancing on1) because of the perception that they are more connected rhythmically.

Rule 3 shatters this argument. Every sound is in clave. This means that there is not one sound *more* in clave than another. Here's another way to look at it. There are five clave beats. One of them plays on the 1 beat, another plays on the 2 beat – which one is more in clave? The point is that clave does not revolve around "one beat." It is the total experience – rule 1. It is the full expression that is important. This is why the 1 beat is just as valid, and in clave, as the 2 beat – or the 3 beat and 4 beat.

There are those that want to separate the downbeats from the upbeats. They make the argument that dancing in clave is separate and contrary to the downbeats – meaning the 1 beat and 3 beat. They want to separate the clave from 4/4 timing. How can you do that? Can you separate night from day, hot from cold, male from female? Without the upbeats you wouldn't have the downbeats. In fact, you wouldn't know what upbeats were if you didn't also have downbeats. This polar relationship is also expressed between the 4/4 pulse and the clave pulse. Without 4/4 timing you wouldn't have the clave as we know it. Clave and 4/4 timing are integrated and essential to each other. The other point to this is that the clave not only plays on the 1 beat and the 2 beat, but also on the 3 beat and 4 beat.

Clave does not distinguish one of its accents as "deeper" than the other. Clave just is. Every accent has equal weight and importance.

Here is another similar argument, worded differently, but saying the same thing in attempting to justify that dancing on2 equals dancing in clave. This quote is taken from the internet.

All the musicians align themselves with the clave. Since dancing is the physical expression of music, if we want to be like one of the instruments, we should also be aligned with the clave. Therefore, the clave binds salsa dancing to salsa music.

Dancing on 1 is not aligned with the clave. It doesn't put you in the clave rhythm. It's more dancing on the melody. The pulsating movement is on the downbeat. Dancing on 1 has no correlation with the clave.

What this quote "really" brings out is that many people do not know what the clave really is and what is its relationship to the entire musical sound. The fundamental understanding that is lacking is that clave *is* the music. The music *is* the clave. You cannot separate one from the other. Everyone gets polarized on those five clave beats and they don't realize that everything in a salsa song is an integrated extension of the clave.

Let's breakdown this quote: Yes, it's true that musicians align with the clave because every sound in the music is in clave. To align to clave means the same as aligning to the music. It follows then, that if every sound is in clave, than every beat is in clave.

The clave binds salsa dancing to salsa music. This is a perfect example of someone trying to "sound" like they're saying something deep. The line itself betrays the person's ignorance. There is no difference between the music and the clave. Essentially, the music and clave are one. The

51

music is the clave, and the basic step connects to the music via the 4/4 time structure of the music – so the 4/4 time structure is the link between the dancer and the music (or clave). The correct statement would be: 4/4 timing binds salsa dancing to salsa music. Or put another way, 4/4 timing binds salsa dancing to the clave.

The line that dancing on 1 is not aligned with the clave has no substance behind it. What is the purpose of one of the clave beats being on the 1 beat? In a way, you can't blame the dancers for perpetuating this idea. They hear over and over again, from the so-called "knowledgeable ones," that on2 dancing is dancing in clave. What is lacking is the critical analysis, which hardly anyone bothers with. It's much easier to just parrot a simple and profound-sounding line than to really examine its true validity. Ultimately, dancers are more interested in dancing than in deep investigations.

We now come to one of the most misrepresented elements of this argument – the melody line. The melody line is perceived to be "outside" of the rhythmic base of the music – thus, not rhythmically connected or rhythmically weak. The main reason for this type of thinking is due to the idea that, hierarchically speaking, the melody sits (or plays) over the rhythm section – some say on top of the music. This idea of being over the rhythm, or outside the rhythm, gives the impression that it is not as connected.

In order to make sense of this you have to understand the function of the various musical components. The rhythm section is the heart of the band. It is the foundational support through which the rest of the instruments can play and improvise and further the intensity of the overall sound.

The role of the rhythm section is to provide the rhythmic basis and foundation for harmony and melody. If you didn't have harmony and melody you would have only drumming or percussion sounds. It would lack musical variety. Melody as expressed through trumpets, trombones, singers, and vibes, is what gives salsa music its creative diversity and enhances the rhythmic drive. Where would salsa music be without singers and brass instruments? There would have been no mambo sound of the 50's and 60's without these elements.

A melody line, by its very nature, and role, is there to create a musical pattern that is not as grounded and as rhythmically consistent as the conga drum, or bass line – the bottom foundation of the music. You can look at melody lines, and improvisational lines by singers (called soneos in Spanish) as equivalent to footwork by the dancer. When you see a dancer doing fancy footwork, she is doing the same thing that a melody line does – using the rhythm section as a means of creating fun and complicated step patterns that go with the basis of the rhythm. The same way the dancer uses the rhythm section to create steps in "clave," is the same way the melodic instruments use the rhythm section to create sounds in "clave." Melody is integrated with the entire musical sound. This means that to fit correctly with the music, the melody must also be in clave. It must be in harmony with every other sound.

It is really a segregative and narrow-minded viewpoint to think that a melody line is less important than a conga rhythm. Every instrument, from conga to a vocal, is serving the musical sound. Each sound is serving its purpose. It is not even a matter of which one is more important. It's like saying, which is more important a brain cell or a liver cell? Each is serving the integrity of the whole. And this is what the clave is really all about. It is the essence and core through which "every" sound revolves around. Clave is the great unifier. Unfortunately, in trying to justify the on2 equals clave idea, dancers have made it a great divider.

It is obvious that what makes us want to dance is rhythm – the foundational sounds laid down by the conga, bongos, timbale, bass and piano. That is the essential factor that makes salsa music what it is. But the rest of the melodic instruments are also integrating rhythmically with the rhythm section, while adding the elements of melody and harmony. Melody and the rhythm section are two parts of the same musical expression. They both complete and complement each other. Just listen to any of Tito Puente's classic mambo songs and you'll realize that the total sound is pushing the music. The total sound is in clave.

It is much easier to dance to a conga pattern than to a melody line. Why? Because the conga plays a basic rhythmic pattern that is consistent and repetitive over one measure of music, and is easily anticipated. Melody, on the other hand, has greater variety in its rhythmic interplay. And, as such, is not as easy to anticipate. When understood in this way, it is closed- minded and limiting to compare, say, the role of the conga drum with the melody. Ultimately, when you really see what this music is all about, these quotes become a play on words whose only aim is to stroke the ego. It betrays a lack of true understanding of what clave is and its relationship to the music and the dancer.

#2

This is taken from a website dealing with the New York on2 salsa scene:

The 2 beat in the 2-part of the clave is the dominant beat of the clave because it resolves the 3-part of the clave. That's why dancing on '2' is dancing on clave.

The weight of this claim rests on the validity of the statement that the 2-part of the clave "resolves" the 3-part of the clave. It then concludes that this makes the 2 beat dominant and, thus, makes the 2 beat equal to dancing in clave.

The obvious question is: does the 2-part of the clave resolve the 3-part of the clave? In order to answer that question you have to understand what is meant (or implied) by "resolving." Musically speaking, resolution refers to a progression from a dissonant to a consonant sound. - from tension to relaxation. Clave is based on reciprocity, or a call and response structure. If you listen to clave by itself, you will realize that the relationship between its two halves is both one of complementing and completing. Both sides can be heard to complete each other. Each side *resolves* the other. The reason for this is because both sides of the clave go together like day and night, hot and cold, male and female. You can't have one without the other. So, does the 2-part of the clave resolve the 3-part of the clave? Yes. But, the 3-part of the clave *also* resolves the 2-part of the clave. And this sense of resolution is not one of an ending or finality, but of a progression, like breathing in and out, that completes and complements, and continues.

This also means that this cycle of rhythm does not make one half more dominant than the other. In fact, each side is dominant in its own way. The statement claiming that the 2-

part of the clave is the most dominant is a weak attempt at explaining that dancing on the 2 beat equals dancing in clave. Both sides of the clave are strong and necessary and equal in their own right. Remember rule 1, even though the clave is broken up into two parts, its power lies in its complete sound. Based on all this, this explanation cannot be used to justify on2 as dancing in clave.

As an example of how these arguments are not thoroughly thought out, let's turn this argument around. If we did agree with the logic of this argument, you can make the case that if you hear the 3-part of the clave resolving the 2-part, it would then make the 1 beat dominant. So if you dance on1 you are dancing in clave.

#3

This next reason is taken from the same source as #2.

So although we don't literally step on every clave beat, we do make a major body movement (a change of direction) on the major beat of the clave, the 2 beat which resolves the tension. It is in this sense that we dance on clave. This style of dancing accents the clave's emphasis on the 2...

Again, the claim here is that the 2 beat of the clave is the one that is more "emphasized," and is the major beat of the clave. We've already determined that it is not. Every beat of the clave is as important and as "major" as the other. Remember, depending on how the musical phrasing in the music is arranged, the 3-side of the clave can "resolve" the 2-part, and vice-versa.

The reference to the "major body movement" is simply the natural back and forth movement that every salsa basic step has.

#4

This is taken from an article on the internet entitled, *The History of Dancing in Clave*. The chart below was used in the article.

Counts	1	&	2	&	3	&	4	&	5	&	6	&	7	&	8	&
Clave	X				X				X				X		X	
Letters	C				L				A				V		E	

The L beat (see chart above - the L refers to the letter which is the beat between the 2nd and 3rd beats) is slightly behind the actual 2 beat. But if you disregard this fact, for all practical purposes the L beat falls on the 2 beat. Therefore, when the man steps forward (left foot) he's stepping on the 6 beat...on the 2 beat (Clave L)...(my underline).

In order to justify that on2 dancing equals dancing in clave, the author is willing to change the placement of one of the clave beats – the L beat. Because it is a half beat away from the 2 beat, the author has no problem moving it over that half beat and saying, oh, it's really the 2 beat. But, there's only one big problem: it is **not** the 2 beat. You have changed the clave. Try playing the clave like that. Statements like this boggle the mind. The exact placement of each of the clave beats is essential to its rhythmic expression.

Can you see what the author of this argument was trying to do? By moving the "L" beat over to the 2 beat, the author can then say that the clave plays on the 2 beat in both of its measures – on the 2 side of the clave and on the 3 side of the clave.

This is a perfect (and blatant) example of force-fitting and disregarding the integrity of the clave to try to validate an idea.

The sad part about information like this is that people will actually read it and believe it, or, at the very least, create more confusion about it. Another sad note to this is that this statement has not been corrected or taken out of the article. It's been on the web for years, and last time I checked, is still there.

How did the "2" Beat get Associated with Dancing on Clave?

The previous four reasons represent the strongest and most "coherent" arguments given to prove the clave/on2 idea. And as can be seen, when examined carefully, they are all flawed. In fact, you come to the realization that the representation of the clave and the basic step were altered and manipulated in order to force-fit their arguments. The bottom line is that none of the reasons given prove that dancing on2 equals dancing in clave. At the very least, we can conclude that dancing on2 is *not* the exclusive way to dance in clave. But we are still left with the fact that for over fifty years this idea has been perpetuated. Why?

In order to answer this we need to go back to the origins of this idea. We have to go back to the historical climate of that time (the mambo craze of the 50's in New York), as well as to the mindset of the musicians who were pushing the on2/clave idea.

In New York City, during the late 40's and through the 50's, a musical transformation was taking place. Afro-Cuban rhythms were merging with innovative jazz harmonies. New York City, particularly in El Barrio, was a fertile ground for musicians, arrangers, and vocalists. Through their creative and collaborative efforts, a new sound was evolving. That sound was vibrant, electrifying, and swinging – and above all, it made you want to move. This sound would eventually take the country by storm and get a whole generation of Americans on the dance floor. That sound? Mambo (later to evolve into salsa).

World War II was recently over, and the country was riding a wave of optimism. The economy was on the upswing, the baby boom movement was under way, rock and roll was taking off, and a sense of stability and "good times" was in the air. Tito Puente, the great bandleader and timbalero, back from the Navy, enrolled in the Juilliard School of Music with the help of the GI Bill – as did many other musicians. Of course, what better way to express this sense of optimism and good times than through music and dance. The general population was ripe for a new and exciting sound, and an earthy and exciting dance to match it.

As the music's popularity increased, so did the number of dancers. Everyone wanted to dance mambo. The sound was new and exciting and as the music evolved in rhythmic intensity, so did the steps and movements of the dancers.

It should be noted that a major influence in dancing mambo was swing dancing, which was very popular at that time. Some of the elements of swing dancing were transposed right into mambo. One of these elements was the creative footwork - what would become known in mambo circles as "shines" or open footwork. Another strong element of swing was the breakaway – where the man breaks away from his partner to go into more dynamic patterns and turns. Swing also had a strong back beat, emphasizing the two and four beats – which is also dominant in salsa music, and would become a contributing motive for dancers dancing on2.

An interesting note is that during the 50's, dancers were not doing many turns and patterns. Instead, there was a lot of solo dancing, where the man would break-off from his partner, and both of them would come up with their own creative steps. This is how many of the dancers of that era danced.

But, the key ingredient to this new mambo sound was the Afro-Cuban rhythms – the drum! Two key features of these rhythms are that they are poly-rhythmic and syncopated. This means that its primary rhythmic accents are playing "off" the downbeats. All the musicians knew this. They knew that the key to this rhythmic flavor and sound was syncopation – particularly as it is expressed from the clave. This is what excited and inspired musicians and dancers. This, then, becomes the essential motivating factor for getting dancers off the 1 beat. The idea was simple: how can a dancer reflect the syncopated rhythmic identity of this music? Answer: by getting "off" the downbeat.

With this in mind, musicians and percussionists began influencing dancers to make a slight adjustment to the way they were dancing. It was based on simple logic. Take the four beats of the music and eliminate the downbeats (the 1 and 3 beats). That leaves the 2 and 4 beats, which are the syncopated beats of the 4/4 time signature. They are also the two beats the conga rhythm emphasizes. The 2 beat is the obvious choice because it begins one of the clave measures and is also one of the beats the conga drum plays. Many songs are played in 2-3 clave, where the clave begins the 8 beat phrase playing on the 2 beat. That was it. That was all the thinking required to say to the dancers: take your main step, your breaking step, on the 2 beat!

Moving the breaking step to the 2 beat was the only shift the dancers made in their dance. Everything else the dancer did remained the same. Of course, there were innovations in the dance as well as the music. All the innovations in the music were based on turning up the rhythmic intensity. After all, this was dance music. The musicians intuitively and/or consciously were always doing it for the dancers. The innovations in the dance came by matching the intensity of the music with body movements, creative footwork, and dynamic partnering patterns.

This shift to the 2 beat, while a simple adjustment captivated and excited dancers. Dancing on2 became an extension of this new musical sound. It became such a rage that dancers would be chased off a section of the dance floor if they weren't dancing on2. At the famous mambo club, the Palladium Ballroom, during the 50's, there was a designated "hot corner" where only on2 dancers were allowed. But what must be understood is that it was at the same time, just another way to connect to the music. What threw a wrench into this on2 thing is when the musicians came out and said to on2 dancers, now you're dancing in clave. This brings us to the heart of the matter. Why did they say that?

When a musician said you're in clave if you're dancing on2, he didn't say it because he put any time in analyzing the basic step or clave. It was said out of sheer impulse and inspiration. What better word to use than the word that encapsulates syncopation and the essence of this music. Clave says it all. It says that if out of the four beats in the music, it was the 2 beat that lifted the dance to a simplistic dimension of syncopation — then in the minds of those musicians; the 2 beat was "closer" to what the clave represented. There was no other way to define dancing in clave. That would actually take some thought. The 2 beat was it. And if you wanted one word to represent what dancing on the 2 beat meant in relationship to the music, what word would you use?

The other point to be made is, if dancing in clave is associated exclusively with dancing on2, then where does that leave the other ways (or beats) to dance salsa? It is this exclusivity that has perpetuated a sense of superiority and authenticity in the minds of on2 dancers. Unfortunately, this idea has also perpetuated a biased and negative attitude toward other dance styles.

In summary, the idea that dancing on2 meant dancing in clave was completely arbitrary. On its own, it had no validity. It was just an opinion. It was an idea that captured the spirit of a time. The music was clave, the clave was the music, and outside of the "sound" of the music, the other integral representation of that sound were the dancers. The on2 movement was new, just like the mambo sound was new. It had to be identified with something extraordinary. It had to be identified with clave.

What is Dancing in Clave?

Because the music is clave, and clave is the music, what does it mean to "dance in clave?"

The problem with this question is that as soon as you define it, you have at the same time limited the experience of the clave. Should we make the basic step the focal point of what it means to dance in clave? If you eliminate the "dancing on2 equals dancing in clave" idea, how do we then define it? The answer is there is no definitive answer.

There are partner dancers that have a good sense of musicality and body movement, and are able to shape and modify the basic step to express themselves – while keeping perfect timing. Is this dancing in clave?

There are solo dancers who move very nicely to the music without any particular basic step. Are they dancing in clave?

Let's compare two dancers. One dancer has very nice body movement and musicality, keeps perfect timing and dances on1. The other dancer is stiff, has no musicality, but dances perfectly on2. Which one is in clave? Or is one more in clave than the other? These questions stimulate us to begin to see how arbitrary it was to say dancing in clave is dancing on2. It also allows us to see how limiting our definitions can be.

Is dancing in clave a combination of your basic step with how you move and style? Over the years there has developed an established way of moving and styling various aspects of the dance. The better dancers are able to incorporate these body movements and gestures, while keeping perfect timing. But the majority of dancers don't have that facility. The majority of dancers are average – they maintain their timing and execute their patterns, and they enjoy themselves as well as anyone. Where do they fit into the clave question?

Let's begin to answer this question on the most basic level - that of feeling. Before you move or dance to the music, you feel the music. "Feeling" the music is the first step in dancing in clave. It is a feeling that connects from your heart to the music and by extension, to your partner. Ultimately, this is all that is needed to "dance in clave." It has nothing to do with dancing on1 or on2 or on3 or on4. It is an expression of your own heart. Dancing in clave is dancing to the music. It is comprised of body movements and gestures that flow in a certain harmony with the timing and accents of the music. Notice, I haven't said anything about the basic step yet. This is because you don't need a basic step to connect in this way.

If we base dancing in clave with our basic step, then we can make the following deduction. If clave is in harmony with 4/4 time, and each of the 4 beats of this 4/4 timing is in harmony with clave, then whatever basic step you use will be dancing in clave. For most dancers this means that if you're dancing on1, you're in clave; if you're dancing on2, you're in clave. If you're dancing on3, you're in clave. Why? Because every part, every beat, every sound of the music is in clave. It is all there for your expression and connection. There is no need for limitations.

Clave encompasses the full musical expression. There is not one sound out of clave. Therefore, in whatever way you connect to the music, you are connected to the clave.

An interesting side note to this is that, in reality, dancers don't bother with clave. In terms of connecting to the music, dancers only concern themselves with stepping on a specific beat with a specific step. Almost all dancers are concerned with executing cool moves and keeping good timing, and putting in some styling here and there – but they are not really thinking about how they relate to the clave. The reason for this is that having a so-called clave sense is really having a "salsa music" sense. Most dancers, especially beginner to intermediate levels, are concerned with maintaining their basic step and executing moves. The idea of clave never enters their mind. More advanced dancers flow with the music (which is clave!) and put style and expressive movements into it, but still don't consciously consider the clave.

How do you feel the music? The music is an extension of the clave. So, to feel the music is to feel clave. Dancing to these Afro-Cuban based rhythms is a subjective experience. If you feel the clave, how can someone else tell you that because you're not stepping on a certain beat with a certain foot that you're not with the clave? Remember, it is the overall bodily expression that creates the togetherness with the music, and by extension the clave. It is not just your feet, but your shoulders, hips, head, hands, and arms. It is opening yourself up to the rhythms, using your basic step as a springboard.

Too much emphasis has been put on the basic step. The basic step was developed to give you a vehicle and structure to partner dance. Within this context, it gave shape and form to the look and flow of the dance, as well as to the partnering possibilities. The basic step was just that – a base, or springboard you can use to fit in what you feel. Let me give you one example of this. When you do a shine step (open footwork done solo) that has a nice flow and is syncopated, what have you done? You have gone beyond your basic step to create a feeling with the music. On another level, you didn't need a basic step for that. Were you in clave?

Unfortunately, the basic step has become the focal point which dancers have used to force-fit the idea of clave into. And that limits the clave's potential. This basic step polarization is a natural outgrowth of the attention and importance that it is given when you take dance classes. Most instruction is basic step intensive, with little explanation or exploration of the rhythmic elements in the music. You are given the steps and the count and that's it. Every now and then someone will mention clave or the *tumbao*, but more as a means of inspiration than for learning. There is no real understanding that is imparted of how your steps and the clave really relate to each other. In fact, instructors will mention the clave or *tumbao* to justify why their basic step and timing are better. The mentioning of the clave becomes lip service for their ego.

As you become an advanced dancer, and work on your body movements and understanding of the music, you will attain a certain command of the timing and your basic step. This will allow you the freedom to play and accent your movements and steps with the music on a deeper level. This is the place where dancers should strive for and takes connecting to the music (i.e. clave) to the next level.

Here is another interesting idea. As the foundation of this music is African based, then to take an African point-of-view regarding the role of music may give us another insight into clave and dancing. From the African perspective, music and dance is a form of meditation. It is a means to connect to spiritual forces. These include ancestors and deities. The object for the dancer is to go into a trance state, to alter her consciousness. In this sense, we can say that these dancers are in clave. The music and their spirits are one. Did it matter that they used a basic step? No. Did it matter that one specific beat in the music is being stepped on? No. While this example can seem far-removed from salsa dancing, it gives us another perspective in the connection between music and dance, and the consciousness of the dancer.

Let's take this last example and use it in a more practical way. I have seen certain men and women who, when dancing, you can see that their basic step is not totally consistent. They're switching beats here and there. They don't know any cool turns or patterns. But, they have a beautiful smile on their face. Their bodies are grooving with the music. Their shoulders shimmy nicely at the right times. The joy on their face is the reflection of the connection of their heart to the music. Are these dancers in clave? I would say yes! Ultimately, your heart is the true connector. These people were obviously not driven by ego. They were driven by the love of dance and connecting to this inspiring rhythm.

Ultimately, connecting to the music comes from the heart. And if that feeling is true, then how could you not be in clave.

Regular rhythm puts us in order – encoded in this language of rhythm are the patterns of our own existence

PART 2

The 2 Beat

The 2 Beat (On2)

Since the 1990's, the most controversial and most heavily debated topic about salsa dancing has been about dancing on the 2 beat, or dancing on2. The controversy revolves around the claim that many on2 dancers make: that dancing on 2 is the "true" way, or more rhythmically connected way, to dance to salsa music. This, in turn, has lead to an on-going rift between on2 dancers and other styles of dancing salsa, particularly on1 dancing. It should be noted that the two most popular ways to dance salsa is on1 and on2. It is this idea of authenticity, along with its sense of superiority that non-on2 dancers want to set straight. For example, on1 dancers argue that their way of dancing is just as rhythmically connected and as authentic as on2 dancing.

While the arguments supporting the claims of the on2 style are few, there are two points that have provided the greatest weight: its history, which includes a strong tie to the mambo craze of the 50's, and, the claim that dancing on2 is dancing in clave. This last point is explored in depth in the Clave Section. For now, it is important to mention that associating dancing in clave with dancing on2 is what has lifted on2 dancing above all other styles. It has created a fascination and mystique that has and continues to captivate dancers. The result of this claim is that it has given on2 dancing the exclusive rights to the master key of salsa rhythms and music – the clave. From the perpetuation of this one idea has come all the controversy, confusion, and mystery regarding the superiority and authenticity of on2 dancing.

Despite all this, the on2 style has grown from its roots in Cuba, to New York City, to numerous countries and cities around the world. The on2 style continues to captivate dancers. This chapter will reveal everything there is to know about dancing on2.

What Does it Mean to Dance On "2"?

For a complete overview of this topic, see the chapter on the Basic Step. Here is a quick explanation:

Your basic step has two breaking steps. Breaking on "2" or dancing "on2" means that those breaking steps (left foot forward and right foot back) are being taken right on the 2 beat in the music. This translates into stepping on the counts 2 and 6 when you're counting to 8. Keep in mind, the count of 6 is still the 2 beat when you're counting by 4.

There are two ways to dance on2. One version, called Palladium Style, is counted as 234-678, with the breaking step starting the basic step directly on the 2 beat. The second version is referred to as New York On2 Style, and is counted as 123-567. In this style, the basic step begins on the 1 beat in order to take the second step (the breaking step) on the 2 beat. Both of these styles are valid ways to dance on2.

The following charts will better illustrate the relationship between the breaking steps and the 2 beat. The breaking steps have a bold **X**. As you can see the bold **X** is falling on counts 2 and 6. If you follow the 4 count, the breaking steps all fall on the 2 beat - thus, on2.

Note: the following are the two basic steps you can use to dance on2. In both cases the breaking steps are taken on the 2 beat.

ON2 – 123-567

Measures	1				2				3				4			
4 Count	1	2	3	4	1	2	3	4	1	2	3	4	1	2	3	4
8 Count	1	2	3	4	5	6	7	8	1	2	3	4	5	6	7	8
Basic Step	X	X	X		X	X	X		X	X	X		X	X	X	

ON2 – 234-678

Measures	1				2				3				4			
4 Count	1	2	3	4	1	2	3	4	1	2	3	4	1	2	3	4
8 Count	1	2	3	4	5	6	7	8	1	2	3	4	5	6	7	8
Basic Step		X	X	X		X	X	X		X	X	X		X	X	X

When did Dancing on the "2" Begin?

It was in New York City during the 1950's, the heyday of the mambo craze, that on2 dancing became firmly established in the United States. Even though they were already dancing on2 in Cuba, it was in New York that a new generation of dancers took the dance to another level and created a momentum for on2 dancing that extends to this day.

Many of the dancers of that time didn't know why they were supposed to dance on the '2', but if they wanted to be with the hip crowd, they had to make sure the 2 beat is where they danced. In fact, over 50 years later, dancers, particularly in New York, are still experiencing this same trend – not really knowing why, but realizing that if they want to be with the "best," they better do it on "2." It was during the 50's that on2 dancing and "mambo" became married. On2 dancing became the "right way" to dance mambo. This was the origins of the idea that dancing to mambo meant dancing on2.

No one knows who was the first one to dance on2. What is known is that they were already dancing this way in Cuba. But, in New York, it was the musicians who pushed the dancers to the 2 beat. They were the main catalyst in the beginning of the on2 movement. Why musicians? Because they understood the music. They understood that the main ingredient in the music was its syncopation – playing "off" the downbeats. And the dancers responded to that. As more and more dancers converted to the "2", they in turn influenced other dancers. After a while the on2 crowd grew strong enough to establish a legitimate on2 movement. It became so popular, that dancers from all walks of life wanted to learn how to dance the mambo, on the 2.

Why Did They Choose the 2 Beat?

It all comes down to simple logic. The way to dance mambo was set. You had the partner dancing with the basic step structure supporting it. The question was: how do you take the basic step structure "as it is", and bring it closer to that idea of syncopation – that idea of playing "off" the downbeats. What came out was the simplest and most straightforward solution. Take the same basic step and move it so it starts one beat later – not on the 1 beat, which is a downbeat, but on the 2 beat, the upbeat, also known as a syncopated beat (the 2 and 4 beats are the syncopated beats within the 4/4 time structure). By the way, the basic structure that was used in those days was the same structure that you see on1 dancers use today – where the basic step starts right on the breaking step.

Of the four beats you can dance on, there are two downbeats and two upbeats. The 1 and 3 beats are the downbeats, or the usually stressed beats in a 4/4 time structure. When you accent a beat that is usually weak, like the 2 and 4 beats, you create syncopation. When the conga player accents the 2 beat by creating a dry slap sound, that is syncopation. When the conga player plays the two open sounds on the 4 beat, that is also syncopation. When a dancer takes her main step of the basic (the breaking step) on the 2 beat, she is dancing on a syncopated beat.

This is the key to why musicians and dancers were excited about dancing on 2. For them it was "cool" to take that breaking step with the slap of the conga. Because these Afro-Cuban based rhythms are poly-rhythmic, it was a way to hook into that "idea" of syncopation - to get off the 1 beat and take it to the syncopated beat. It was this simplistic adjustment that injected a refreshing and invigorating enthusiasm to the dance, which in turn, matched the refreshing and invigorating new sound called mambo!

Because of this, musicians and dancers would say "now you're dancing to the clave." Why? It was because the clave is the essence of the music – the essence of that syncopation. It seems like a major exaggeration to bestow such an honor on a dance because you shifted your step by one beat. The idea of dancing in clave was not based on any musical secret - it was just some musicians' or dancers' inspired opinion.

The point to understand is that shifting to the 2 beat was not anything so "deep" or special, but rather, it was just different, and it provided a different point of reference to the music. The net effect was that it excited and inspired the dancers.

Another side note to the upbeats (the 2 and 4 beats) was that during this time period (the 40's and 50's) swing music was popular. One of the main musical features of swing was its strong backbeat - the backbeats being the 2 and 4 beats. This trend continued through jazz and pop music.

This is how "on 2" dancing took hold in New York. It's important to keep in mind that all of this evolved informally. Initially, the basic step was developed to connect with a partner and the 4/4 timing of the music, without any concern for any beats or rhythm. Then, someone came up with the idea to have the main step of the basic fall on the 2 beat.

The Two Basic Steps for Dancing On 2

Today, many dancers recognize the two basic steps that are used to dance on the 2 beat. The first style is referred to as Palladium style or the ballroom 2. The other basic step, that has become popular due to Eddie Torres in NY, is called the NY 2, or street 2. They are also identified by the counts in the music they are associated with: the 234-678 for the Palladium style, and 123-567 for the NY 2.

It is important to realize that outside of the way these two basic steps begin, four out of the six steps are the same (the 2-3 and 6-7 steps). It would seem that they have more in common than not.

History of the basic step on 2

One of the biggest misunderstandings regarding these two basic steps has to do with how each one originated. Let's take a look at where each of these basic steps came from.
How did the 2-3-4/6-7-8 on the "2" start?

The first basic step people used to dance mambo on2 was the so-called Palladium step or ballroom 2, where the counts are 234-678. This was the basic step structure that emerged out of the *danzon* and became the way to dance the various styles of *son* as well. This is also the basic step that emerges out of the streets of El Barrio in New York during the 40's and 50's. The emphasis in this basic step is that it starts directly on the 2 beat or the breaking step. But remember, the structure of the basic step was a way of connecting to the underlying 4/4 timing of the music, without any thought to clave or specific beats. This basic step was also used by dancers to dance on1.

How did the 123-567 on the "2" start?

This step was developed in the ballroom dance studios of the 1950's. Yes, many dancers are not aware of this. The reason that they developed this basic step was because so many people were having trouble finding the 2 beat and starting directly on it. Which in the 50's, starting right on the 2 beat (skipping the 1 beat) was the authentic way to dance mambo. Beginning on the 1 beat to step on the 2 beat is similar to the way the studios created a preparation step for starting the cha-cha-cha basic. When you take the first step on 1 it is in preparation and anticipation of stepping on the 2 beat with your breaking step. Also, before the mambo, ballroom studios were teaching the *rumba*. The studios took the basic *son* step from Cuba and made it into a box. Of course, they started on the 1 beat. It was easier to get people to dance if they started on the 1 beat. This was the idea behind this 123-567 mambo basic as well.

The idea was that if you can hear the 1 beat, then you will find the 2 beat. It makes sense because, naturally, two follows one.

This basic step was featured in Life Magazine, dated December 20, 1954. In this issue there is a picture sequence with the caption, "basic step is done to eight counts." There are eight pictures with explanations of each step and what count is being taken. It clearly shows the 123-567 basic being done. The writer of the article went to the popular dance studio of the time to get this information.

In the 50's and 60's, the Palladium style basic (234-678) was called 'street style," and the NY2 (123-567) was considered the ballroom 2. Today, it is the reverse. Palladium style is considered ballroom, and the NY2 is considered street style. Knowing this history will allow you to see how, over time, the perception of dance styles can reverse and contradict itself.

Differences between the Two On2 Basic Steps

Besides the differences already mentioned, there are a few others that you need to be aware of. Because of the sequence and position of each basic step, and where the pause step occurs in each, there is a certain amount of variation in getting into and out of patterns and turns. This includes where you might put in styling and body accents.

For example, in doing double-turns, the 123-567 basic allows for an easier preparation time than the 234-678 basic. Another example is when women go into the "copa" step. This is the NY name for this move. It is just a curl-type step where the woman will do a half-turn to her left coming out of her back basic and then goes back out on her left floor like a regular cross-body lead. When doing the 123-567 basic, the woman has 2 beats to make her half-turn. In the 234-678 basic, the woman has only 1 beat to do the half-turn, which means she has to move quicker to do the pattern. These types of differences in how much time you have to begin or end a dance pattern determines also differences in how the lead is executed.

In general, the 123-567 provides an easier approach to getting into patterns because the basic step begins on the 1 beat, which means that there is an extra beat for preparation. This is why you will hear many dancers comment that this basic gives you more time in your dance. In general, the 234-678 basic gives a little more time in the end part of the patterns.

Another point to each basic step, and dancing in general, is that as you get better you will attain a certain amount of command that allows you to make adjustments for turns and styling. This means that you can break out of the rigid restraints of the basic step (at certain points) and timing to accommodate a more efficient way (or it could just be putting in some styling) to do certain turns or patterns.

The point to take from all this is that even though there are differences that alter when the lead and follow take place, whatever you can do with one basic step you can do with the other. It doesn't make one better than the other. It's about what a dancer prefers based on how he/she feels the music. Unfortunately, so many dancers, especially in New York, take their basic step way too seriously. They become prisoners of their basic step. Wouldn't it be great if you say - for this song I'm feeling a 234-678, or I'm really hooking into the 1 beat so I'll dance "on 1." Or, the 123-567 basic on the 2 feels good here. Can you see the possibilities? You're dancing by feeling and fun rather than by dogma. It must be remembered that the basic step is only a springboard for what you are feeling inside. Any pattern, turn or whatever can be done with any basic step.

How the 123-567 Became More Popular than the 234-678 Basic

During the 80's, when interest in mambo/salsa dancing was low, there was one dancer/performer who took it upon himself to teach and keep the dance alive. This person was Eddie Torres, from New York. The basic step that he was teaching was the 123-567 on the 2. By the 1990's, mambo/salsa was beginning to get popular again and Eddie Torres' dance classes were also increasing in popularity. Overtime, some of his students became advanced dancers and went out on their own as instructors and performers. It was this propagation of instructors, going through what would become known as the "Eddie Torres style,". that popularized this basic step in New York, as well as other places around the world. Because Eddie Torres was an independent instructor, this style was also categorized as a "street style." It is important to understand that what made Eddie Torres appealing to dancers was not the basic step, but the creative steps and dance patterns that he taught. Again, you must realize that a basic step is just a springboard for your dance. Everything that is done on the 123-567 basic can be done on the 234-678 basic, with minor adjustments.

The popularity of the 123-567 basic is typical of any popular trend: when enough people do it, and do it well, and when they truly believe in what they're doing - it will influence others to join in and be a part of that experience. As during the 50's, so it is today: dancers want to be with the other "hip" dancers. It is this perception that creates a movement. Today, more and more dancers want to "crossover" and learn the on2 style. In NY, you have a saturation of independent instructors and studios that are teaching the 123-567 basic. This continues to reinforce its popularity even more.

The reason that the 234-678 basic is known as the ballroom 2 is because it has always been taught in the ballroom studios – going back to the

1950's. The ballroom studios would always go to the clubs and watch the best dancers. This is how they kept up with the latest dances and moves. Of course, the best dancers were the so-called street dancers. The studios would take what they saw in the clubs and create a structure to teach it. What is ironic is that it was the ballroom studios that came up with the 123-567 basic step. This is the same basic step that is referred to as street style today. As rock-and-roll came in during the sixties, interest in mambo dancing, and partner dancing in general, waned and the ballroom studios dropped the modified basic step (123-567) and continued teaching and dancing the original version of 234-678.

Following is an excerpt from a book on mambo dancing that was published in the early 60's titled Latin Dancing:

...a slight change will be introduced to the rhythm to capture the feeling of syncopation which is the difficult part, but also the thrill of the real mambo. We shall start all our steps on the count of four (where the pause used to be), thereby anticipating the down beat (count one). Since we are ahead of the music, we shall then pause after having taken our first step. The pause will take place on the count of one. The counts of two and three remain the same. There, you have what makes the mambo "the mambo"...

What this excerpt is elaborating on is how the authentic mambo is danced 234-678, when the pause is on the 1 beat. This is the ballroom 2.

Is Dancing on2 the Best Way to Dance?

Yes and No. Why? Because it is all totally subjective. For some it is, for some it isn't. There is no way to measure how much any one person is feeling the music. Ultimately, it doesn't matter how you dance as long as you are inspired! Really, dancing is about feeling and moving. If a person is on the dance floor, moving and grooving beautifully, and is dancing on1, then what is that saying?

Dancing on2 is a preference. It's another way you can dance to this Afro-Cuban based music called salsa. There are many, many dancers that love it, but there are also many, many dancers that love dancing on1. This is the bottom line: after a night of dancing and you have that semi-spiritual feeling of joy and satisfaction – you feel great – what does it matter, at that point, what beat you were dancing on.

So, Why Dance on the 2?

Dancing on2 is another way to connect and express yourself to this music – via the basic step. Some dancers love the idea of taking the breaking step with the slap of the conga. They love the idea of dancing on the syncopated beat. But dancing on2 comes with a mandatory requirement – the conscious awareness of timing. In order to dance on2 you have to know where that 2 beat is. That sounds obvious, but it is a difficult challenge for many dancers. It is for this reason that on2 dancers tend to be more knowledgeable about the music and timing than other dance styles. Having a greater awareness of the music develops a deeper understanding of the rhythmic components of the music. That can only help make you a better dancer. Another benefit of learning on2 is that once a dancer knows how to dance on2, it will be easier for him to dance on any other beat. This is not the same for on1 dancers. It is more difficult for an on1 dancer to dance on2.

An interesting aspect of learning to dance on2 is that most beginners and non-2 dancers feel an awkwardness dancing on the 2 beat. The natural tendency of the music makes them want to step on the downbeats. They're not used to taking their steps at that point in the music – especially if they've been dancing on the 1 beat, or some other style. Dancing on 2 is an acquired taste. It takes a little time to get used to that feeling of stepping at that point in the music, but after a while it will feel as natural as dancing on1. The following are some of the reasons dancers decide to dance on 2:

They are inspired by other dancers who rave about it.
The only classes available in their area are on2.
They want to hang with a certain dance crowd and they all dance on2.
They see great dancers at a club, and of course, they're dancing on2.

What these four reasons allude to is that for the majority, if not all dancers, wanting to learn on2 is initiated outside of themselves. It isn't something that happens naturally from hearing the music.

It must be made clear that dancing on the 2 beat is not superior to other ways or beats to dance on, and it does not connect you any "deeper" into the music, and it does not automatically mean you are dancing "in clave."

An interesting aspect of dancing on 2 is that the 2 beat is actually a weak accented beat within the context of the whole musical sound. This is another reason why it is difficult for many people to find the 2 beat, and why the NY on2 basic uses the 1 beat as a reference to find the 2 beat. In fact, the 4 beat, where the double open sound of the conga is played, is a stronger accent, in general, than the 2 beat. And, of course, the 1 beat has the strongest pull of all the beats – which is why all dancers, before they take classes, will dance on1.

Another incentive related to learning how to dance on2 is the inclusion to not just the social world of salsa dancing, but even more exclusively, to the social world of on2 salsa dancing. It is a natural human tendency to want to belong and be accepted by a group – in this case the on2 group. And this is perfectly normal and fine. The only drawback with this is that there is a tendency to become exclusionist, and at worst, snobbish. When this happens the whole idea of what dancing is all about is lost, and dancers make the basic step and beat they dance on their main purpose for dancing– turning some dancers into on2 salsa Nazis.

My contention is that it's fine that you want to dance like all the "best" dancers and be part of a group thing, but really, dancing is a subjective experience. There must come a point where dancing on the 2 beat is happening because it is the way YOU want to connect to the music, and not just because you want to fit in with others. This is a point that is hardly considered by on2 dancers.

For example, as a musician and listening to salsa from the 60s' and 70's, I naturally hooked into the bass line and breaks that accented on the 4 beat. I learned to dance on2 but I found that dancing the 234-678, on the 2, allowed me to step on the 4 beat and express those accents through my dance. While I also learned the 123-567 on the 2, it didn't provide the expression that I was naturally hooking into. I was able to make this choice because of my appreciation and feeling for what I connect to in the music. It's not just about counts, and it's not just about following the crowd. But, I also enjoy dancing on the 123-567 on the 2.

Although instructors and dancers get caught up in trying to find "deep" reasons for why dancing on the 2 beat is superior to dancing on other beats, the truth is that there is no legitimate reason that makes one way of dancing better than the other. Connecting with clave or the rhythms comes from the heart – not your steps. In fact, you don't even need a basic step to connect to the clave and the music.

Finding the 2 beat

There are two ways to work with finding the 2 beat. The first method is to know how to find the counts in the music. This requires that you find the 1 beat within the 8 beat phrase (see the *Timing Section* for more information on this). Once you find the 1 beat you will know where all the other beats occur. This was the logic that the ballroom studios used in coming up with the 123-567 basic on the 2. This is an accurate way of knowing at all times where you are in the music.

The other way is to listen and feel the rhythmic phrasing without using any counting. This is a more difficult way to dance on2. It is all feeling. Most dancers who dance this way do not maintain their timing 100% of the time.

I recommend that you learn how to count. This will insure that your timing will always be accurate. After you master your counting you can then drop the counting and incorporate more feeling into maintaining your timing.

Things **not** to rely on in finding the 2 beat:

Listening for the singer and *coro*. This comes from the idea that the singer and *coro* in many songs will start on the 1 beat. The problem with this is that there are songs where they are not coming in exactly on the 1 beat. When you are looking to master your timing you want to make sure that you have accurate references in the music that will work all the time. That accurate reference will always come from the rhythm section.

Listening for the clave. The clave is not played in most salsa songs, but it is always implied. The most accurate way to find the 1 beat is to learn how to hear the 8 beat phrase in the music. You don't need to know anything about the clave in order to do that.

Most dancers who dance on the 2 will learn where the 1 beat is and from there find the other beats. In fact, it is the count that most dancers will hook into to stay on the 2 beat. This is due to the approach all the instructors take in teaching on the 2. They concentrate exclusively on counting for all their instruction. Unfortunately, this has its good and bad points. What happens is that you have a mass of dancers who are constantly counting in their heads while they dance. But, to really master your timing, you need to be able to connect with the underlying rhythmic sounds of the music. Doing this will take you deeper into the music as well as improving your timing tremendously. It also means that you have to wean yourself from counting. It's ironic that dancers spend a great deal of time learning to count to maintain their timing, and when they have it mastered, they then need to stop counting.

Usually, most dancers never eliminate the mental counting. It's always there, though maybe more in the background.

Transitioning from dancing on1 to dancing on2

There are many dancers making the transition to dancing on2. Here are some points and guidelines:

Do your best to <u>only</u> practice and dance the on2 step and timing – until you get it. You are trying to reprogram your steps, which can become confusing if you keep going back to the old way you danced. If you do continue to dance both styles, it will take you longer to get the on2 timing, and in some cases, you may never get it.

You also have to transition the way you listen to the music. If you've been dancing on1 for many years you have gotten used to "hearing" the music to dance on1. This means that you not only have to change your steps and what beat they are on, but just as important, you have to change the way you "hear" and reference the music.

To set a good foundation for learning I suggest a deliberate and progressive approach. For example, do the basic step with the counting (without any music) until there is no thinking about it. You have to make sure that the counting is nice and even and consistent. It's important at the beginning to count every beat – this means counting like this: 1-2-3-4 5-6-7-8 1-2-3-4 5-6-7-8, and so on. This way you will make sure that each step is taken at the right time and are also accounting for the beat (the pause steps) you don't step on.

Practicing this way will strengthen the muscle memory needed to get the step pattern down. Once the basic step is going good, include turns, shines and even partnering – again, do it with only the counting.
Next, do the same thing, but now using only the conga drum rhythm, or *tumbao*. Keep counting until you are a 100% sure of where your steps fall

in relation to the conga accents. This is a key exercise because it not only reinforces your basic step pattern, it also draws you into the basic rhythmic pattern of the conga drum and you begin to feel and hear how your steps integrate with those sounds.

Be patient and very deliberate. At times you might feel like you've never danced before. This is normal. You just have to keep at it and don't skip any steps.

On2 Mix of Sayings and Proverbs

If you're in or around the on2 world you'll come across what I call on2 proverbs. These are sayings passed down from musicians and dancers that reflect a sense of superiority and greater rhythmic connection for on2 dancing. Many of these sayings are used to justify why dancing on2 is better and belongs to an elite group. For the rest of this chapter we will take a look at the most common of these sayings and see if they have any real merit.

Note: some of these sayings refer only to a specific basic step (the 123-567 or the 234-678), while others refer to both. We begin with the first saying that contrasts on1 versus on2 dancing.

Dancing mambo is on2, dancing salsa is on1.

This is another one of those sayings that, when you really understand it, is based entirely on perception and not on reality.

See the introduction on the explanation of the labels "mambo" and "salsa."

During the 50's, both mambo music and on2 dancing came on the scene at around the same time. Because of this, they were logically linked together. But, what must also be understood is that there were many dancers during that period that danced "mambo" on1. Because the music of mambo came before on2 dancing, most dancers were dancing on the 1 beat or 3 beat – which was perfectly natural. Even during the entire mambo era of the 50's, compared to all dancers, there were still only a small percentage of them that were actually dancing on2.

So before the word "salsa" came on the scene, there was already a connection and history between mambo and on2 dancing. Dancing on2 became associated with mambo because enough people (dancers and musicians) pushed that idea, and after a time it became set in their minds that mambo and on2 dancing go together like, well, rice and beans. An idea became a belief. This mindset is what sets the first half of the saying, "mambo is on2," in place.

When the label "salsa" came on the scene (during the early 70's), like mambo, it at first identified only the music. And of course, in a short amount of time it also came to represent the dance. The question now becomes, how and why did dancing on1 become synonymous with dancing "salsa."

Here are a few factors that created the perception that dancing "salsa" was dancing on1."

1. There were a group of musicians who resented calling the music salsa. Tito Puente being the most prominent one - which was why he always said, "salsa I eat, mambo I play." It's not much of a stretch to translate that into "salsa on1, mambo on2."
2. The label salsa became very popular. It soon became an umbrella name for all kinds of Latin music and dancing – which was definitely not mambo or salsa as we know it.
3. In the 70's and into the 80's, the majority of dancers dancing to "salsa" were on1 dancers. This was not only in New York, but also internationally. By the 70's, on2 dancing had died down, and at the same time a new movement and generation of dancers were beginning to dance salsa – mostly on1.
4. The sound of the music was different. The classic mambo sound that is associated with the 50's made it that much more identifiable with the

92

on2 experience. By the 1980's the music was much more commercialized and diluted. This was the beginning of the "salsa romantica" sound.

It is obvious that this saying, "mambo on2, salsa on1," was started by either a "mambo" dancer or musician, who knew the "tradition" of on2 dancing. In the eyes of many who "knew" this tradition, it was important to keep that history, that tradition, that on2 "truth" alive. But to keep it alive meant that on2 dancing could not be associated with this new movement called "salsa." In their minds, on2 dancing can only be associated with its rightful mother – mambo. This was the mindset that created the mambo on2, salsa on1 idea. A side note to this is that the "salsa" movement was what sparked and reinvigorated the interest in this music and dance, which led dancers to the classic mambo/salsa sounds and the rediscovery of the on2 styles.

The implication that salsa produces on1 dancing and mambo produces on2 dancing is a false one, and not based on the reality of the music or dance. Take the music - on2 dancers were dancing to the same music that on1 dancers were dancing to. In fact, 99.9% of all dancers who never got training of any kind – listening to the mambo sound of the 50's or the salsa music of the 70's – would start dancing on the 1 beat. It wasn't until someone made them aware of dancing on2 that they changed their way of dancing. So there is nothing inherent in the music (both of the 50's and 70's) that makes you want to dance on one beat more than another.

The music continued to evolve after the 1950's. The NY sound of the late 60's and 70's was a continuation of the rhythmic drive the music had coming out of the 50's. The big bands of the 50's had given way to smaller bands, called *conjuntos*, with a mixture of two to three trumpets or trombones. Eventually, through a marketing effort, that sound would be called "salsa." The so-called "mambo" dancers were still dancing on2 to this music. The music of the 50's (called mambo) and the 70's (called salsa) had as its foundation the same rhythmic intensity. Ultimately, the labels salsa and mambo could be used interchangeably when referencing the dance.

Dancing on the 2 beat is dancing to clave

The chapter on the clave should be read to get a complete overview of this topic. If you know what the function of clave really is, then you will realize that a basic step falling on the 2 beat does not give you the exclusive rights to dancing on clave. Nor does any form of "on 2" dancing mean you are dancing more in clave than dancing on any other beat.

Dancing on2 fits the structure of the music better

Let's take the 123-567 basic first.

It is said of the 123-567 basic that it "logically" fits the rhythms and therefore it matches the strongest rhythmic components of the music. It is explained that this happens because you are stepping on the 1 beat, which is a strong beat, and you break on the 2 beat, which goes with the rhythms of clave and *tumbao*. The idea is that you are hooking into the full power of the rhythmic structure of the music. The problem with this argument is that it has imposed an analytical, logical, mental approach to a feeling, spirited rhythmic dance. It is like what Luis "Maquina" Flores says, one of the greatest dancers during the Palladium days, "nobody cared about numbers or beats, they danced to feel the music, and let the music take them to move their shoulders, hips, arms, whatever."

It all comes back to the understanding that dancing is about connecting with your heart, not a step. This is the key that has been lost on many dancers and instructors. Yes, you need to step. Moving your feet is the foundation of movement, but that should not be the total focus.

It is true that the 1 beat is the strongest of the 4 beats within the 4/4 time structure. This is the reason that everyone who starts dancing (before they take classes) will always start on the 1 beat. However, it must be understood that the role of the first step on the 1 beat (for dancing on 2) is transitional and used as a "preparation" for stepping on the 2 beat. It does not really "power" the basic step. The fact that it falls on the 1 beat is incidental to hooking into the music. The structure of the basic step is such that the real power, or emphasis, falls predominantly on the breaking step. In this case that would be the 2 beat. Of course, there are moments in the dance where you will accent on the 1 beat. For example, just before going into a breakaway position the dancers can do a slight counter-body extension on the 1 beat before going out into the cross-body-lead on the 2 beat. This is a hesitation movement that creates a nice dynamic for moving into the cross-body-lead. However, the main accent for this basic step falls on the two breaking steps (left foot forward and right foot back).

The other side to this argument is that, in reality, dancers do not dance the way this explanation makes it sound. In general, dancers don't put any more emphasis on their breaking steps than any other step.

Also, when you take into consideration that the reason this basic step came into being in the first place was because people were having a hard time dancing directly on the 2 beat, you begin to see how, over time, new ideas were created to validate the premise of greater rhythmic connection.

The step on the 1 beat was simply a preparation step to get to the 2 beat because most people were not used to hearing and hooking into these Afro-Cuban rhythms. It was easier to start on the 1 beat to then step on the 2 beat.

If we take the logic of this saying, then we can say this about any beat we dance on, with any basic step. For example, we can start our own basic step. You can start on the 4 beat with your right foot, which is the strong *tumbao* accent, and then take your breaking step forward on the left foot on the 1 beat, which is a very strong beat. Then, we can step on the 2 beat to finish. In this way we will be stepping on three very strong rhythmic beats. Why not? You can justify anything.

By the way, this same reasoning applies to the 234-678 basic as well. This step does not "logically" fit the music anymore than dancing on any other beat. In other words, each basic step for dancing on the 2, as well as the basic for dancing on the 1 beat, all fit the logic of the music as much as the other. Remember, the basic step developed to fit the logic of 4/4 timing and that's it.

The 234-678 basic

The 234-678 basic fits nicely with the conga rhythm, or *tumbao*. The basic step hits both main accents of the conga. That said, you must remember that this is just another way to connect with the music. It is not the end all or be all of connecting to the music. If the conga is where you like to connect, fine, dance with it. If not, then dance on something else, because dancing is an integrative process. Every sound in the music is a way "in" to establishing a connection. Your steps and the music are an interplay, a call-and –response relationship, where the heart is the primary connection.

You are more rhythmically connected on the 2 beat

We need to understand that the basic step was developed to hook into the underlying pulse of 4/4 timing. In reality, the clave and *tumbao* interplay with this underlying 4/4 timing, which means that every beat is rhythmically connected. Every beat harmonizes with the clave. Every beat harmonizes with the *tumbao*. Every beat harmonizes with the melody. Which means that whatever beat you're dancing on is as much "in clave" or "rhythmically connected" as any other! If you want to hook into the conga, great, then step on the 2 beat and the 4 beat – which means you'll be doing the 234-678 basic on the 2. But keep in mind, just because your step is matching a beat that the conga is playing does not make you more deeply rooted in the music, or more connected. If you want to hook into the cowbell on the downbeats, that's great too, find a basic where you can step on the 1 beat or the 3 beat. The fact is that you don't have to step directly on any beat to be connected fully to the music. Why, because all your steps and your body movement are integrated with the music.

We need to step out of this narrow-minded thinking about isolating "a beat" within the full musical expression and making it the god of all beats. You will be missing the forests for the trees. It's ok if you really enjoy dancing on the 2 beat, with whatever basic, but don't think that that makes you more connected, or rooted deeper in the rhythms. Your first and true connection from where you are truly connected in clave is from your heart. From there your movements will reflect and express that primal connection.

Dancing on 2 is dancing in the rhythm,
dancing on 1 is dancing to the melody

By creating a contrast between the rhythm and the melody in a musical arrangement, the creator of this saying is betraying his ignorance of the function of a musical arrangement and its relationship to the basic step. This was explained more fully in the *Clave Section*. If a melody line is in clave, which if it is properly arranged it should be, does this not mean that it is as rhythmically connected to the clave as any other musical element? Many swinging piano lines (*guajeos* or *montunos*) have their strongest accent on the 1 beat. Does this mean that it's not as rhythmically connected because it's not accenting stronger on the 2 beat? Can you see the foolishness of this? The piano line is swinging because it is weaving its sounds with the clave and with the rhythmic impulses. This is exactly what happens with the basic step. Your steps, your heart, are weaving and playing with the conga, with the piano, with the bass, with a trumpet line, with the coro. It's all good! You do not have to step directly on a beat the conga is playing to be "in" the music.

Dancing mambo was created on2, and thus the only way to dance Mambo

No. Mambo dancing became associated with dancing on2 by certain groups of dancers and musicians during the 1950's. This established the on2 movement, which in turn gave birth to the idea that dancing on2 meant dancing mambo. You have to understand that this all evolved informally. The majority of dancing was done on1. Over time, as the word of on2 dancing spread, and enough dancers were doing it, did the idea that mambo should be linked with dancing on2 became established.

You hear the 1 beat and feel the 2 beat

You can feel every beat. And you can hear every beat.

The 234-678 basic is the true power 2

In order to deal with this we have to understand what "power" refers to in your basic step. Generally speaking, the power in your basic step centers on your breaking steps – left foot forward, and right foot back. It is there, where there is a change of direction and weight, that you can create a greater dynamic in your dancing. The reason this basic step is referred to as power 2 is because there is a pause step before you step on the breaking step. This means that you have two beats to prepare to take your breaking steps - left foot forward and right foot back. That extra beat enables you to generate more energy into that 2 beat - thus, power 2. This basic step was the most popular way of dancing during the on2 movement of the 50's and 60's. The breaking steps would also be referred to as charge steps because you can "charge" into them – creating more accent and intensity.

That said, you must realize that this "power" can be generated with either of the two basic steps used to dance on the 2 beat. Again, it is a matter of each individual putting "in" to the dance what they feel and not necessarily the basic step structure. This means that the real power is originating in the heart and attitude of each individual dancer.

On2 is a more sophisticated way to dance

We have to agree on what is meant by "sophisticated" to address this line. It seems to indicate that just knowing where the 2 beat is in the music elevates your level of sophistication. To a certain extent it is correct. You do have to know where the 2 beat is at all times. But, a person could be dancing on2 correctly but have awful body movement. It doesn't seem that this type of dancer could be considered sophisticated.

You can consider on2 dancing as sophisticated in the sense that your ability to hear the music is more refined. You do have to cultivate a musical awareness that enables you to maintain your timing.   Although, you can have knowledgeable dancers who know the music well and still dance on1. A good example of this are musicians.   They know the music but when it comes to dancing they just go totally with the feeling, which in most cases is the 1 beat.

Sophisticated can refer to your technique as a dancer. It can also refer to how you are able to play off the music and your partner that goes beyond doing typical dance patterns. Therefore, to say that dancing on2 is more sophisticated may feel that way for some dancers and not for others. This expression of sophistication can be applied on the 1 beat as well. This being the case, it is a totally subjective experience, which means it is not valid as an overall definition.

Dancing on 2 hooks into the tumbao, which is the heart of the rhythms

If you use this argument for dancing on the 2, then you would want to dance on the 234-678 basic, or the Palladium 2. Why? Because you're able to step on the 2 beat *and* the 4 beat, which are the two main accents of the conga.

If you're dancing the 123-567 on the 2, then you are stepping on only one of the accents that the *tumbao* plays – obviously the 2 beat or slap sound of the conga.   On this note, I have heard an instructor who teaches the 123-567 basic on the 2 say that he was a natural 2 dancer. He said that he used to practice just hearing the *tumbao*, and step right on that slap. This was before he knew anything about where the 2 beat was or had taken any classes or formal training.   When you examine what he said closely it makes no sense. If you really hook into the conga drum you will find that it is counter-intuitive to start dancing on the 1 beat to step on the slap, or 2 beat. It is not a natural feeling to do the 123-567 basic to just the *tumbao*. Take any person who has never taken a class and ask him/her to step on the slap of the conga, and see what basic he/she starts doing. It will be the 234-678, where you start the basic right on the slap, or 2 beat.

The conga drum pattern is considered the heart of the rhythm because it sets the rhythmic foundation for the music. This is the role of the "bottom" instruments – to set a consistent rhythmic pulse for the rest of the musical expression.

While the *tumbao* may have been an impetus for dancing on 2, it does not mean that it is the only rhythmic reference that you can hook into. As was stated before, it is the interplay between the various rhythmic sounds that give the music its drive and swing. The point is that this interplay of sounds is working and harmonizing together to create this rhythmic pulse to dance. Your basic step is part of this interplay. So whatever beat you dance on, you're still going to be grooving with the conga rhythm. It is a dance of pulses where every beat is valid, every beat is necessary, and every beat harmonizes with each other. And your heart is the real portal to connecting to these rhythms.

Tito Puente says you dance mambo on 2

To understand why Tito Puente would say this is to understand the mambo scene in its heyday - the 1950's. As was mentioned in the beginning of this section, all the hip dancers had to do it on2. At the Palladium Ballroom, there was a "hot corner," where all the best dancers showed off their best stuff. You had to be on 2 to even get in the corner. The 2 beat was cool to dance on because out of the 4 beats you can "break" on, this was the closest to syncopation that you can get to, while dancing with a partner. It was this one step that put the stamp on New York mambo dancing. This is similar to how New York put its own stamp on the mambo sound. As Tito

Puente was a vital part of this era, he naturally championed this way of dancing wherever he went.

The point here is that just because Tito Puente says it, does not mean that it is right. But, you can understand why he says it. There is a distinction between the mambo sound of the 50's, which Puente helped to define, and the salsa sound that came out of the 70's, 80's, and 90's. In this sense one can understand Puente's desire to define his sound with the label "mambo." In the 50's, dancing on2 was a way of distinguishing dancers from all others. Dancing on2 defined a "new" dance that went together with the "new" sound called mambo. Tito Puente understood this and this is why he never wavered from this idea.

PART 3

The Basic Step

THE BASIC STEP

If dance is a universal language, then the basic step is the vocabulary through which we can speak to each other through movement.

The basic step is the common language that allows two people to converse through movement. It is the "basic" connection to the music and to your partner. But, it is also a gateway where you can bring out a wide range of bodily creativity and expression.

The mambo/salsa basic step is unique in its versatility and ability to hook into the Afro-Cuban rhythms that are the foundation of salsa music. It is versatile because you can use it for both partner dancing and solo dancing; for both dancing elegantly and dancing funky and earthy. It provides a unique balance between European and African dance expressions.

The basic step is relatively simple – 3 steps forward and 3 steps back. Within a few minutes anyone can start dancing the basic step with music. But what is especially great about the basic step is that its simplicity allows dancers to be as creative and expressive as they want to be. And it is the creativity of the dancers, through the springboard of the basic step, that has allowed the dance to grow and evolve over the last fifty years.

A prime example of this is the way the dance evolved in the 1950's. Because of the intensity of the mambo sound (fast and furious), dancers began to improvise over the basic step structure. Dancers would spontaneously create all kinds of steps. You would see everything from Cuban *rumba*, to tap dancing, to African dance, to early forms of break dancing. This type of dancing was an urban extension of *rumba* and *son* dancing that was taking place in Cuba for decades. That the basic step lends itself to such a wide range of possibilities is one of the reasons that this dance is so exciting. Keep in mind, when I refer to the "basic step," I am not referring to any specific basic step, but rather to the general basic step structure (3 steps over 4 beats).

It was also during the 50's that the idea of "shines," or solo footwork started. Over time instructors took some of these improvised steps and gave them names, and then taught them in their classes. This is how the standard group of "shines" came about. Today, most classes start with solo footwork and body styling as warm-ups before they go into partner instruction.

The other contributing factor that has influenced the "flavor" of the dance is the fact that this music is African based. It is drum music, clave music. It is music that is steeped in earthy, entrancing rhythms. And it is these rhythms that have drawn out the gestures and movements that are associated with this type of dancing, and which breathe life into the basic step.

The basic step is a springboard for expressing yourself. It is a template that supports a full and rich expression of movement. It is a logical structure whose sole purpose is to connect your movement to your partner and the music. On a deeper level, it connects your heart to the music and to your partner. Ultimately, your movement, and your steps are all about feeling and connection. And it is this feeling, emanating from your heart that animates your dance.

Origin and Evolution of the Basic Step

No one can say for sure exactly when and where this basic step first came on the scene. There are dance forms that have a similar step and timing structure – 3 steps and a pause – over 4 beats - each step and pause getting 1 beat. In fact, a similar step is seen as far back as the 16th century in a French dance called the *Branle*.

We do know that the structure of the basic "salsa" step emerges within the Cuban dance, *danzon*, which in turn, evolved out of the popular dance and music called *contradanza*. It is in the *danzon* that we clearly see the mambo basic step figure. This is the step that will also be incorporated into dancing the "Son," which was another musical form that evolved in rural Cuba – later to be known in the United States as *rumba*. In fact, this basic step structure is the one that the majority of Latinos will use in dancing to Afro-Cuban based music. What is this bas ic step? It is the quick-quick-slow structure that is associated today with dancing on the 1 beat. It is also the structure that on2 dancers doing the "Palladium style" use, counted 234-678.

This basic step migrated to the United States, and specifically New York City, during the early part of the 20th century. During this time, there were two factors that propelled this basic step to greater popularity. The first was the increasing number of Latinos migrating to New York City (particularly Puerto Ricans who were allowed to freely enter the United States under a modified status of citizenship), and the second was the *rumba* craze that began in 1930. It was out of this *rumba* craze that the ballroom studios took the raw basic step Latinos were using and modified it to make the steps accessible to the general public. They took the basic step and converted it to the *rumba* box step, while maintaining the basic

3 steps over 4 beat configuration of the street version. By the 1940's the ballroom studios would make *rumba* a standardized ballroom dance.

This brings up an important association between the ballroom studios and the street dancer. The studios would take the creative patterns and steps of the street dancer and codify it and teach it in a structured format. It is this unofficial association that helped to popularize the dance. Without the creative input of the dancers, the dance would stagnate, and without the structure of the studios the dance would not be accessible to many potential dancers. Unfortunately, over the years, there has been a certain antagonism between the two groups. But, they have both played, and continue to play, an important role in keeping this dance alive. In fact, as we shall see, it is the ballroom studios that developed the popular basic step used by on2 dancers today – the 123-567 on the 2.

The dominant basic step that emerges in New York at the advent of the mambo scene in the late 40's and 50's is the quick-quick-slow form, where you start the basic step directly on the breaking step, either forward or back. This is the basic step that the majority of dancers are familiar with, and for Latinos, this is the step that their parents and family members were doing at parties and celebrations. The majority of dancers during this time were dancing on the downbeats – the 1 and 3 beats. As the dance and music developed the idea of moving the breaking step to the 2 beat (which was already taking place in Cuba) came into vogue and the beginning of on2 dancing came into being. This is the on2 basic step that today is known as the Palladium style. This was the basic step that most of the dancers were doing during that time. But, as was mentioned, another basic step developed to help dancers get the 2 beat - this is the 123-567 on2 basic developed by the ballroom studios. This basic step will reemerge in the 1980's in New York City through the efforts of an independent instructor named Eddie Torres.

The important point to understand about the genesis of the basic step was that it was an intuitive and informal process. Through the influence of dance structures that had evolved up to that point, dancers found a way to adapt step patterns for their partnering to match the demand of the music.

In New York during the beginning of the mambo craze, there was no concern for what beat you were dancing on, or whether you were in clave or not. Dancing was a social outlet to get away from the daily grind of work and life's turmoil's. Connecting with the music came from the heart, not from what beat you took a step "on."

The main "timing" factor in the development of the basic step

To understand how musical timing influenced the development of the basic step structure, you have to understand that there are two rhythmic pulses going on in the music. The first is the 4/4 time pattern and the other is the syncopated Afro-Cuban rhythms – such as the *tumbao* rhythm of the conga, or the rhythm of the clave. The 4/4 time pattern is the foundation over which the Afro/Cuban rhythms are built.

In order for dancers to connect their movement in a way that can make sense, it was intuitively realized that their steps had to connect to the most stable and consistent timing pattern in the music. In other words, the basic step could not be based on the syncopated aspect of the music. It could not consider the *tumbao*, or the cowbell, or the cascara rhythm.

The most important timing consideration for the basic step was that each beat of every measure of music has to be exactly the same – which is what 4/4 timing provides. And this exactly matches the requirement for partner dancing – that the follower's steps match (or mirror) the leader's steps exactly. This repetitive, alternating step pattern is what gives the dance the symmetry and logic that makes all the turns and patterns of the dance work.

The Role and Function of the Basic Step

The role of the basic step is to provide the structure and logic to communicate – to have a conversation through movement. In this way, both leader and follower know exactly where they are in relationship to each other and to the music. This is accomplished through the symmetry of the basic step – the forward half taking the same amount of time, and steps, as the back half. This creates the relatively simple logic that dictates when the follower can turn, and where the leader can turn, and where the leader can bring her into a cross body lead, and so on. It provides the logic to execute all the patterns and combinations that make up this dance.

The basic step is the foundation and key to every aspect of your dance! This means that everything you do – from simple turns, to complicated turn patterns, to intricate footwork - always has the basic step underlying it. What this also means is that <u>a key to being a better dancer centers on how much command you have of the basic step.</u> This point cannot be emphasized enough because many beginners want to learn patterns and turns but fail to really master their basic step.

From the previous sections we can summarize the function of the basic step as follows:
1) to allow you to connect with the music, via timing and tempo (4/4 pattern)
2) to allow you to connect with a partner through its structure (step pattern)
3) to provide a springboard to express yourself

Anatomy of the Basic Step

This breakdown of the basic step applies to the two most common basic steps today: the first is dancing on the 1 beat and the second is dancing on the 2 beat. The following are the common attributes of the basic step:

1) the basic step is made up of two parts: a forward half and a back half
2) for the forward half – the main step is the left foot forward (this step is also known as the breaking step)
3) for the back half – the main step is the right foot back (this is the other breaking step)
4) you take 3 steps and a pause for the forward half and three steps and a pause for the back half.
5) each step takes up 1 beat, and each pause takes 1 beat
6) the complete basic step takes 8 beats to complete.
7) there are 2 breaking steps – one for the forward basic – the left foot forward and one for the back basic – the right foot back.

The basic step can be danced in various directions – back and forward, side-to-side, circular. It generally depends on where in the world you are located. The linear, slot-oriented approach is the style most associated with New York on2 dancing.

Counting the Basic Step

The full basic step (forward half and back half) takes place over 8 beats. For this reason, the best way to count the basic step is using an 8 beat count. Another reason to use the 8 beat count is because the music is written and arranged in 8 beat segments. So counting to 8 not only helps you connect to the music, but it helps in developing a greater awareness for the different rhythmic elements in the music.

Counting to 8 while dancing to salsa music is the most efficient way to keep time.

Using the 8 beat count gives each step of the basic a unique number. This makes it easier for learning dance patterns, as you'll know by the count what step you should be on. But, you should realize that counting is really for instructional purposes and after you have a good command of your timing, you want to wean yourself off the mental counting.

Here's an example of counting the basic for the 123-567 on2 style. In this style, you start the basic on the 1 beat. From the leaders point-of-view, he would start back on the left foot on the count of one. The back basic would continue with the right foot back on the 2 beat, and then back on the left foot on the count of 3. What follows is the pause step, on the count of 4, where there is no weight change. The forward basic would continue with the counts of 5-6-7 and then the pause on the 8 beat. This way of counting allows you to incorporate the 3 core principles that are covered in the timing chapter.

Breaking Steps

There are two breaking steps in your basic - one for the forward half and one for the back half. The breaking step for the forward half is on the left foot. The breaking step for the back half is on the right foot.

<u>The breaking step for your forward basic</u> is when you step forward on your left foot, and from there, you rock back, or change the weight back on your right foot to transition into your back basic. The breaking step stops (or breaks) your forward momentum, and at that point, your movement goes back.

<u>The breaking step for your back basic</u> is when you step back on your right foot, and from there, you rock forward on your left foot to transition into your forward basic.
Again, this breaking step stops (or breaks) your backward momentum and your steps will now come forward.

These steps were also called charges, or charge steps. They called these steps charges because it was also the step that you can put the most energy into, or "charge" into it. The effect of this step is that you can both "charge" into them (by creating momentum), and at the same time they "break" your momentum to bring you to the opposite direction.
It is the breaking step that determines what beat you're dancing on to the music. This means that if you're dancing on the 1 beat, it is because your breaking step is landing on the 1 beat in the music. This will be covered more in depth in the timing section.

What beat do you dance on?

Eventually, as you get more into the dance, someone is going to come up and ask you, "what beat do you dance on?" or you are told, "you have to dance on 2!" You're immediate response is a perplexed look and then, "what?"

Everyone goes through this scenario. Let's start with the obvious question...

What does it mean to dance on the 1 beat, or 2 beat...or...

The answer to this question was touched upon in the previous section. In order to answer this question you need to know two things, and then put them together.

The first thing you need to know is that the music has four beats. One of these four beats is the beat you will dance "on." The second thing you need to know is: what is your breaking step. This was just covered, so hopefully you know where the breaking step occurs in your basic step.

Note, the charts after this section illustrate the breaking steps and their relationship to the beats and the basic step.

Now, we put these two things together. When you say you dance on1, or the 1 beat, it means that the breaking step is falling right on the 1 beat in the music. Remember, you have two breaking steps, so your left foot forward will fall on the 1 beat, and your right foot back will fall on the 1 beat. If you look at the basic step charts for on1 (below), you will notice that all the bold X's fall on the 1 beat – when looking at the 4 count row.

If you're counting to eight, the first breaking step will fall on the 1 beat, and the second breaking step will fall on the 5 beat (this can also be reversed – where you start on the 5 count and the second breaking step will be on the 1 beat). Remember, the beats 1-2-3-4 are the exact same beats in the music as 5-6-7-8 (see the 4 count row).

If you dance on2, then the breaking steps will fall on the 2 and 6 in the count. Both 2 and 6 are both the 2 beat. Looking at the basic step chart, there are two variations for dancing on 2. One is the 123-567 on2, and the other is the 234-678 on2. The important point is that in both cases the bold "X" is always on the 2 count.

If we are dancing on the 3 beat, then the breaking steps will fall on the 3 and 7 in the count. Both the 3 and 7 are really the 3 beat, so you're dancing on the 3.

Basic Step Charts

The following charts show the relationship between the different basic steps and the count, as well as where the breaking steps are. The breaking steps are shown with a bold "**X**".

ON2 – 123-567

Measures	1				2				3				4			
4 Count	1	2	3	4	1	2	3	4	1	2	3	4	1	2	3	4
8 Count	1	2	3	4	5	6	7	8	1	2	3	4	5	6	7	8
Basic Step	X	**X**	X		X	**X**	X		X	**X**	X		X	**X**	X	

As you can see the bold **X** is falling on counts 2 and 6. If you follow the 4 count, the breaking steps all fall on the 2 beat. Thus, on2.

ON2 – 234-678

Measures	1				2				3				4			
4 Count	1	2	3	4	1	2	3	4	1	2	3	4	1	2	3	4
8 Count	1	2	3	4	5	6	7	8	1	2	3	4	5	6	7	8
Basic Step		**X**	X	X	**X**	X	X		**X**	X	X		**X**	X	X	

In this basic, the breaking step begins the basic step, and it begins directly on the 2 beat.

ON1 – 123-567

Measures	1				2				3				4			
4 Count	1	2	3	4	1	2	3	4	1	2	3	4	1	2	3	4
8 Count	1	2	3	4	5	6	7	8	1	2	3	4	5	6	7	8
Basic Step	**X**	X	X		**X**	X	X		**X**	X	X		**X**	X	X	

Notice how the breaking steps fall always on the 1 beats. In this basic step, your breaking step begins directly on the 1 beat.

For all 3 charts, note how there is a beat (or box) in every measure which does not have an "X". This is the hold or pause step in the basic step. In order to stay on time, you need to make sure that you account for this hold step (for 1 beat) before you make the next step.

The Two Most Popular Basic Steps

Currently, there are two basic steps that are the most popular in the salsa scene. For arguments sake I will call the first basic step the universal basic. This is the quick-quick-slow version that is the most universally known and done. With this basic, you can dance on any beat in the music. The majority of people doing this basic will usually dance on the 1 beat. This is the basic step done in the LA salsa scene as well. When this basic step is used for dancing on the 2 beat it is counted as 234-678, and is also known as the Palladium style, or ballroom style.

The other basic step that is used exclusively for on2 dancing is the basic step that is counted as 123-567. This basic step is associated in NY with Eddie Torres, and is loosely referred to as the Eddie Torres style. Because this style is identified with the NY on2 scene, we will call this basic step the NY on2 basic.

<u>The universal basic step – for dancing on the 1 beat, 2 beat, etc.</u>

This is the basic step structure that emerges out of the *danzon*. It is the quick-quick-slow steps that most people dance around the world, and anyone who has ever danced intuitively will always dance this basic step. This is the most popular basic step in the world.

The NY On2 basic step

The basic step, known also as the Eddie Torres style, was developed in the ballroom studios of New York during the 1950's. It was developed because many dancers who wanted to dance on2 were having a hard time finding the 2 beat and staying on it. The idea was a simple one: if you can find the 1 beat, you can then get to the 2 beat – because the 2 beat follows the 1 beat. So the basic began on the 1 beat as a preparation to step on the 2 beat. This was the same idea used in Cha-Cha-Cha, where the ballroom studios used the 1 beat to start the dance in order to break naturally on the 2 beat. More information on this basic step style can be found in the section on the 2 beat.

What Beat do you Naturally Dance On?

Most people (99.9%), if they've never taken classes before, will dance on the 1 beat (or the 3 beat). Why? It is because of the influence of the 4/4 timing of the music. The 1 beat is the strongest accent in the 4/4 timing of the music, and therefore the beat you will naturally gravitate to. The 3 beat is the next strongest beat in the 4/4 time structure which is the reason that dancers also naturally dance on the 3 beat. The 1 beat and 3 beat are known as downbeats. This is a primary reason why many beginner dancers have a hard time learning to dance on2. It is a natural feeling to want to take the main step of the basic on the most stable and strongest accent in the 4/4 structure – the 1 beat. Also, the 4/4 time signature is the most popularly used timing in most music. This includes pop, rock, jazz, Latin, and classical. So the majority of people naturally follow the 4/4 timing dynamic.

Because of the prevalence and strength of the 1 and 3 beats of the 4/4 time structure, it's almost impossible to find a "natural" untrained on2 dancer that's consistent – which means they break on the 2 beat every time. As was mentioned in the chapter on the 2 beat, dancing on2 is an acquired taste, or in this case, an acquired step. Dancing on 2 requires that you "hear" the music in a different way, which means that there is some training of the ear involved to hook into the music in order to find the beats and stay on it.

What Beat Should I Learn to Dance On?

The two most popular beats to dance on are on1 and on2- or the 1 beat and the 2 beat. It is important to realize that one is not better than the other. It is just a preference, which means that both beats are fine to dance on. That said, the question still remains – what beat should you dance on?

The answer to this question is one you must answer for yourself, but here are a few points on the process:

In general, the easiest and most straightforward beat to dance on is the 1 beat. This is the beat that all dancers naturally gravitate to, as was mentioned above. Leaning to dance on2 requires a more conscious awareness of the music and therefore takes more time to master. But, to really master your timing, regardless of what beat you dance on, will require a certain amount of time and effort. You still have to connect with the music in such a way that you "know" where you are in the music at all times. This usually requires that you learn to count the music – which is what you have to do to dance on2.

Where you live will determine what type of dancing you have access to, and what teachers are available. This will also determine the dancers you will come in contact with – which in turn determines what basic step and timing you will be doing. Remember, the idea behind dancing is to connect to the music, connect to your partner, and express yourself. You can do that with any basic, on any timing.

How serious are you? Do you really want to get good? Do you want to make this a regular part of your life? These considerations will determine how committed you are in taking your dancing to a certain level, and in turn, how much time you're willing to put into it.

Regardless of what beat you dance on, or what basic step you use, if you want to dance with good timing, you need to have an excellent command of counting the music. Counting the music is a sure-fire way to know that your timing is 100% accurate. Of course, there are exceptions. There are some dancers that have a natural ability to hear the rhythmic patterns in the music and anchor their basic so that they're timing never wavers. These dancers, however, are few and far between.

In general, on2 dancers, because of the higher demand of being on their timing, are better rounded dancers – meaning, they will be able to dance on any beat. Only someone who has a good command of her timing can do this.

What Basic Step should I Learn?

Usually, people will learn from the instruction that is the most popular and available in their area. Today, there is a greater awareness of the different styles, so you find dancers who want to learn on2 dancing, but live in a predominantly on1 city. These days all the major cities in the US and in various other countries will have both on1 and on2 dance instruction.

The easiest and more intuitive basic step is the one used for dancing on the 1 beat – the quick-quick-slow version, where you start the dance directly on the breaking step. This is also the basic step, that, when danced on the 2 beat is known as Palladium style (counted 234-678). It is more "natural" to start the basic step by stepping out, and then back in with that same step.

To become a "real good" dancer you need to have an excellent command of the basic step. With time and effort you can master any basic step, with any timing. It all comes down to how much time and commitment you have to get there. Essentially, regardless of what basic step you do, it is the inspiration of the music that "moves" you and fills you with a sense of excitement and fun.

Right Brain/Left Brain and the Basic Step

Dancing is a predominantly right brain activity. This means that you feel it more than think about it. This is the way you get the most benefit from dancing. But during the process of taking classes and learning the dance, most people's focus is on "thinking" about it – or the left side of the brain. This is completely natural and the way it should be. But, ultimately, as a dancer you want to free yourself from the mental focus (especially the counting) and turn it completely over to feeling and connecting (to your partner and the music). Unfortunately, once you seriously begin working the timing and counting it is difficult to drop it, especially when you use it to start the dance. It becomes almost like reading. Once you learn to read, whenever you see writing you will read it, whether you want to or not. What this means is that you have to make a conscious effort to continue to "feel" your timing through your basic step in order to allow a more feeling approach.

A great way for beginners to start going with the feeling and connection with the music is by dancing to just the conga rhythm. See exercise 3 in the next section on working with the basic step. Also, when dancing to a song that you can keep accurate timing to, establish your basic with the proper timing and then close your eyes and feel the music and the way your steps are interacting with it. Make a conscious effort to shut off the counting and "listen" to how the steps go with the sounds. This is a great exercise to really focus in on the interrelationship between the musical sounds and your steps.

The right side of the brain enables you to become one with your experiences. It allows you to dissolve yourself into the wave of music and dance. As dancers, this is what we want. We want to lose ourselves in the music and in the oneness with our partner.

Working with the Basic Step

As the basic step is the key to mastering your dance, here are a few exercises that will help you to really get it down. These exercises can be used with whatever basic step you use. What is necessary is that you know the mechanics of the steps, and on what counts you take each step on.

Exercise 1 - Setting a consistent count while doing your basic step

Done without music.

Do this as slow as you need to do it right.

Establish a consistent and even beat. If you have a metronome – good, otherwise you can clap, or use the basic step guide on the timing CD offered in appendix B.

Begin to count 1-2-3-4 5-6-7-8.

Now, do your basic step with your counting – keep it very even, making sure that you account for every beat in your basic step, and that you are accounting for the hold steps in your basic.

Add turns and even dance with a partner – just counting.

What this exercise will do is to reinforce the mechanics of your steps with a consistent count. It will strengthen the muscle memory and the timing in your basic step, so that you can take that same feelings and timing when you do it with music. This will help make your basic step second nature.

Another modification to this exercise is to vocalize with the conga sound.

The 123-567 basic on the 2

We will use what's called Ladies Timing, by starting the count going forward. To get started, we wait for the count "4-and" or the "tuum-tuum sound and then we immediately step on 1 with our right foot.

The following table shows the relationship between the conga sound, the count and the basic step. You can use it as a reference for doing the exercises.

Conga Sound	Count	Basic Step
	1	Step forward with right foot
Pah – Slap	2	Step left foot forward – this is your breaking step
	3	Shift the weight back to your right foot
Tuum-tuum	4 and	Preparing to step back on left foot -
	5	Step back on left foot
pah	6	Step back on the right foot – breaking step
	7	Shift the weight back on the left foot
Tuum-tuum	8 and	Preparing to step on the right foot forward

This is how you would vocalize this first exercise:

Tuum-tuum 1-2-3 tuum-tuum 5-6-7 tuum-tuum 1-2-3 tuum-tuum 5-6-7...
and so on. You can emphasis the 2 and 6 count as those two beats are
where your breaking steps will fall on.

The 234-678 basic step on the 2

This basis step aligns more naturally to the sounds of the conga drum. To
begin, we will step directly on the "pah" or slap sound with our left foot.
An interesting point about this basic step is that you can dance it with the
conga without counting. This is because you're aligning your first and third
steps of the forward and back basic with the 2 accents of the conga on
beats 2 and 4.

Conga Sound	Count	Basic Step
	1	Preparing to step on left foot
pah	2	Step left foot forward – this is your breaking step
	3	Shift the weight back to your right foot
Tuum-tuum	4 and	Left foot steps back to neutral position
	5	Hold and preparing to step back
pah	6	Step back on the right foot – breaking step
	7	Shift the weight back on the left foot
Tuum-tuum	8 and	Right foot steps forward to neutral postion

Notice how in this basic you step directly on the 2 main accents of the
conga rhythm.

Exercise 2 - Doing all kind of shapes with your basic step

Done without music.

As in exercise 1, establish a solid, consistent and even basic step.

Then, begin to play with your basic step so that you can shape it and turn it anyway you want, while maintaining the same count and step structure. Play with making the steps smaller, or wider, step out to the side, cross the steps over, turn in a circle – while maintaining the basic step with the counting. Take your time and allow your creativity to try different things.

This exercise will help you to maintain a consistent basic step with the counting no matter how you shape the steps. One of the problems beginners have is breaking out of the back and forward pattern of the basic step. This exercise will reinforce your basic step so that no matter what you do, you are marking out the basic step with the proper foot at the proper time.

Exercise 3 - Dancing to just the conga drum

This is a great exercise. It not only helps you with your basic step, but it reinforces dancing to a consistent rhythm. Another great thing about dancing to the conga drum is that you can do it with counting, or you can do it without counting. You can do it by just going with the feeling of the rhythmic phrasing. Once you hear and understand the relationship between the conga accents and your basic step, you don't need to count. Your basic step becomes an interplay with the conga accents.

For on2 dancers, dancing to the conga drum is a great reference because the two main accents of the conga rhythm occur on the 2 beat and on the 4 beat. By dancing to the conga, an on2 dancer can dance on2 with 100% accuracy.

The sound the conga plays on the 2 beat is a slap, high-pitched sound. The sounds on the 4 beat are two open sounds – heard as a toom-toom sound. The key for dancing on2 is to make sure the breaking steps (left foot forward, right foot back) land on the slap sound of the conga. Also, for dancing the 123-567 basic on2, you will use the toom-toom sound on the 4 beat to prepare to step on the very next beat, which would be the 1 beat. Remember, in this basic you never step on the 4 beat (and 8 beat when you count to 8).

For on1 dancers you would use the toom-toom sound to begin your basic on the very next beat – the 1 beat. The next step would be the 2 beat, or the slap, and then would come the 3 beat.

If you're dancing 234-678 on2, your breaking step would begin the basic step directly on the slap of the conga, followed by beat 3 and then you would finish your half basic with the step coming back to center on the toom-toom sound, on the 4 beat. In this basic, you never step on the 1 beat and the 5 beat.

Use the charts at the end of this section to see how the basic steps and conga accents interact with each other.

Exercise 4 - the basic with full music

In this exercise you will take a song where you can hear the conga rhythm clearly enough to maintain your basic step without losing the timing. The following are two recordings where the conga drum stands out:

Otra Opportunidad – Jimmy Bosch

Mambo for Vibes – Hilton Ruiz

As you get good with one song, add another and another until you can begin to "hear" the conga even when you can't hear it in the music! When you get to this point you should be able to dance without ever losing your timing. But, it doesn't end there. Mastering your timing is not just about losing your timing. After all, that is only the most basic requirement of dancing. When you have truly mastered your timing you will be able to let go of your steps, you can improvise, allow the music to move you, and your partner. This is the reward of dancing with spirit, while still maintaining impeccable timing!

Remember, you will only get there by putting the time into it. It is through repetition that you achieve mastery.

Also, when dancing to regular music you should be hooking into the 8 beat phrasing, along with the conga rhythm.

Conga/Basic Step Charts

The following charts will allow you to see the relationship between the different basic steps, the counts, and the conga beats. As before, the breaking steps are shown with a bold "**X**". The main conga accents fall on beats 2 and 4. The 2 beat of the conga is the slap sound, and the 4 beat is the open sound. If you use the 8 count, the conga accents fall on beats 2, 4, 6 and 8.

Note that for On2 dancing the breaking steps fall right on the slap of the conga rhythm – this being counts 2 and 6.

ON2 – 123-567

Measures	1				2				3				4			
4 Count	1	2	3	4	1	2	3	4	1	2	3	4	1	2	3	4
8 Count	1	2	3	4	5	6	7	8	1	2	3	4	5	6	7	8
Conga		X		XX		X		XX		X		XX		X		XX
Basic Step	X	**X**	X		X	**X**	X		X	**X**	X		X	**X**	X	

ON2 – 234-678

Measures	1				2				3				4			
4 Count	1	2	3	4	1	2	3	4	1	2	3	4	1	2	3	4
8 Count	1	2	3	4	5	6	7	8	1	2	3	4	5	6	7	8
Conga		X		XX		X		XX		X		XX		X		XX
Basic Step		**X**	X	X		**X**	X	X		**X**	X	X		**X**	X	X

ON1 – 123-567

Measures	1				2				3				4			
4 Count	1	2	3	4	1	2	3	4	1	2	3	4	1	2	3	4
8 Count	1	2	3	4	5	6	7	8	1	2	3	4	5	6	7	8
Conga		X		XX		X		XX		X		XX		X		XX
Basic Step	**X**	X	X		**X**	X	X		**X**	X	X		**X**	X	X	

Putting Flavor into the Basic Step – A Primer with Doing More than just Stepping

Many dancers become concerned about putting flavor into their dance. They want to be able to add nice rhythm and movement to their dance - the so-called "Latin motion." This is especially true for the women.

In general, there is a certain connection and awareness of the body, and the way it moves, that dancers need in order to move their body a certain way. This is one of the most challenging aspects of dancing salsa. As dancers progress they are concerned with looking good and wanting to express themselves in a certain way. Many dancers are self-conscious of their "stiffness."

The most important approach to putting the flavor into your dance is to keep it natural. You cannot force yourself to move in ways that you are not used to or are capable of. It takes time.

The following are some basic movements to get you started in connecting back to your body's ability to move. It would be good if you have a mirror that you can use to check your movements.

Isolations

Shoulders

Move them up and down, alternating them. Circle them, one at a time, and then alternate them. Explore the movements the shoulders are capable of. Practice shimming slowly and build speed.

Once you have this going, begin to do the movements while taking a step forward with your left foot. Only take one step – bring the left foot forward and then bring it back to the start position. Then, do the same thing with your right foot - bring it back and then to the starting position. While taking the step, feel the way the shoulder responds to that movement. For example, when you step forward with the left foot, there is a natural tendency to bring the left shoulder forward. Also, notice how the ribcage also moves in that direction. While looking at this movement in the mirror, see how the upper body relates to the step. Does it look good? Does it feel good? Continue to play and explore with these movements.

Ribcage

Take the ribcage and begin to move it to the right and to the left. Feel as if the movement is originating from the middle of the ribcage. Keep everything else very relaxed. After a while begin to do these side ribcage motions while taking a side step – to the right and to the left.

Bring the ribcage forward and back. And again, incorporate the movement with a simple step.

Hips

Of course, the hips! This is the part of the body that is associated the most with Latin dancing. To loosen up the hips and feel the muscles for that area, warm up with some basic hip movements. This includes hip circles, tucking in your pelvic area and releasing.

Keep in mind that your hips are always involved in stepping. It's just a matter of how much you accentuate the movements. Women tend to be more in touch with these movements than men.

When doing steps, the movement of the hips originate with the action of the knees. This first movement will demonstrate the relationship between the knees and hips. Keep your feet naturally apart, the same distance they are in when doing your basic step. To start, bend your left knee slightly and straighten your right leg. Now begin to alternate your legs: bend the right knee and straighten the left leg. Do this movement slow and play with exaggerating the motion so you can really feel the action of the hips. Again, looking into a mirror helps a lot. A good way to work this movement is dancing to a slow merengue.

The next step is to try it with your basic step, but, take small steps, so that you're hardly moving. Make sure that the leg that's stepping is the one that is bent. You should be producing a swaying of the hips. Keep in mind, this is not the way you are going to dance. It's just a way to feel and be more conscious of your hip movements.

As you explore these movements and continue to work with them there will come a point where they are becoming more natural. You will gain a sense of awareness and control so that you can dance and express yourself in the way you want.

Practice dancing in front of the mirror. Explore the movements of your hips and shoulders. Don't be afraid of trying something new, or of trying a movement you saw another dancer perform. This is a continuous process. You have to dance and explore. In time you will notice changes in your dance.

Other Activities

Any activity that works with movement and body positions will help you. This includes, yoga, other forms of dance (African, Afro-Cuban, jazz, hip-hop, swing, etc), martial arts, and fitness workouts like zumba.

What all these forms of movement have in common is that they help to increase your connection to your body – to bring a deeper awareness, a conscious awareness between your mind and body. It can only help in making you a more expressive and creative dancer.

The Basic of No Basic

The idea behind this "Zen like" concept is that as you master your timing and your dance patterns, you don't have to stick to stepping on every basic step. By mastering your basic step you liberate yourself from it. So although you are maintaining the structure and timing of the basic step as you dance, you can move out of it at any time. There are beginners who look at advanced dancers and say, "I couldn't see the basic step in what you were doing." This level of dancing provides you the added freedom for greater self-expression and creativity. This is what dance is all about!

This is an advanced way of dancing that takes time to develop. In the beginning, the basic step rules every part of your dance. Up to about the intermediate level, everything that you do requires that you account for every basic step. And this is as it should be. But because dance is about feeling and self-expression, your dance continues to evolve. This means that your experience with the basic step also evolves. The more you dance the more you experience a greater freedom: you become very familiar with the turns and patterns and there comes a time when you can feel that there is "time" to do something at a particular moment in the dance. Something different. Maybe it's a little kick step, or an arm movement, or a shoulder roll, or a little jump back. You reach this breakthrough in your dance because you've been dancing a certain amount of time, and experiencing the dance more and more.

But, it's important for you to realize that it only happens when you have reached a certain level of mastery in your basic step, timing, and the way you integrate that with the patterns and turns that you do. This means that if you don't do it enough times you will never get to that point.

Here's a simple exercise to get out of your normal basic step:

1- Start you basic step

2- As you go to do your back basic – instead of stepping back on the right foot, bring your feet together and bend your knees, bringing your body down slightly for the full count of your back basic. This means that you are not taking any steps. If you have to, keep the count going in your head.

3- Go back into your normal forward basic.

What this simple exercise does is to allow you to experience the timing of your basic step without taking every step. It also gives you an experience of how to substitute an example of body styling during the basic step.

Hand-in-hand with this idea of allowing expressive movements is your ability to "hear" the music. It is the music that has to take you to that place of greater self-expression. By feeling the music, you translate that into spontaneous body movements and gestures. It is always the music that drives the dance. Try doing the exercise above with a song that you really enjoy listening to – one that really gets your juices flowing. Then during breaks in the music, or parts that really inspire you, try incorporating a movement, or body gesture, other than the basic step at that point. But, do not lose your timing. You should be able to flow back into where you should be in your basic step. Don't worry about making mistakes and screwing up. The point is to let it happen. Have fun with it and explore the possibilities.

This idea of dancing beyond your basic step is related to putting style into your dance. Style can be defined as the attitude and inspiration you put into your dance that translates into the movements and gestures you perform during a dance. These gestures could be small and understated or big and flashy.

Switching from One Basic Step to Another – Within a Dance

This happens mostly to on2 dancers. And it usually happens when dancing the 123-567 on the 2. What happens is this: a dancer is dancing along fine, doing the 123-567 on2, and then after doing some kind of dynamic turn or pattern, he falls into the 234-678 basic step on2, for a few steps or a few measures of music. Instead of waiting for the 1 beat or the 5 beat, he steps directly on the 4 beat or 8 beat in the count.

Why does this happen? For an experienced advanced dancer it means that the feeling took over. It happened without conscious awareness. To some mambo "purists" this is a big no-no. But is this wrong? Obviously, it depends on what you believe. But if we answer this from the idea that dancing is all about self-expression, then the answer is NO, it is not wrong. As long as you did not disrupt the connection with your partner and with the music (losing your timing) then it is perfectly fine.

As advanced dancers it is important to realize that we should not be slaves to a basic step. You can step anywhere, and do anything, as long as you maintain your timing and don't disrupt your connection to your partner. As long as you maintain the integrity of your connection with your partner and the music, then your dancing is at the highest point it could be! You have to get back to the true reason you dance – to allow yourself to "feel" the music, and to express yourself through your body. Feeling the dance and the music is more important than being a slave to the basic step.

When this happens to a beginner or unsure intermediate dancer it usually means that their basic step is not strong. The point is that you have to master the rules (the basic step) before you break them.

Shines – Open Footwork and the Basic Step

As was mentioned in the beginning of this chapter, the salsa/mambo basic step lends itself to an almost unlimited amount of improvisation and creativity. It is in open footwork that this is reflected the most. There are countless variations that can be done off the basic step.

The beauty of doing solo footwork is that anything goes. You can do just about any kind of step pattern. You can use patterns from jazz, tap, swing, and hip-hop, to name a few. And after the improvised step, no matter how many measures it took, you will always come back to the point in the basic step you would have been if you had just been doing your basic step.

With open footwork you are less restricted. You can spend an entire 5-minute song doing steps that do not resemble anything near a basic step, and it would be all right. There is a greater freedom to explore and experiment with the various rhythmic accents and the specific music you happen to be dancing to. Doing solo work allows you to change basic step timings without any problems.

With partnering, there is a need to maintain the basic step structure, although there are moments and places where improvising steps can be done. But partnering is involved with the lead and follow and the connection between two people – not one dancers self expression.

Practicing with Music that you Love to Listen To!

This is SO important.

I always mention in my classes that you have to dance and practice to music that "really" inspires you. It has to really get your juices flowing. What you feel, which gets reflected in your dance, begins with the music.

Whenever you hear a song that you like, make sure you get the name of it. Build a musical library of songs you really enjoy dancing to, and then practice to them. It makes all the difference in the world.

PART 4

Timing

TIMING

Timing is one of the most challenging elements for many dancers. Yet, the first and most important criteria for being a good dancer, is having solid, consistent timing. Most dancers agree that dancing with someone who can keep time is the most important factor for having a "nice" dance.

What happens to many dancers struggling with their timing is that they "hear" the music, but they have not learned to "listen" to the music. By learning and practicing to listen to key references in the music, any dancer will be able to "hear" how the music relates to the counting, and be able to maintain accurate timing.

What it means to master your timing

On a basic level it means that you can keep time with the music – meaning – your basic steps are falling on the beats that they should. But, <u>mastering</u> your timing is much more than that. When you have truly mastered your timing, besides having impeccable timing and execution during your dance, there is a sense of freedom that allows greater expression, musicality, styling, improvisation and connection with your partner. This all comes about as a result of being in a relaxed and open state of being, where your entire being "knows" where you are in the music. Timing no longer restrains you, but rather liberates you.

The majority of dancers keep track of their timing in one of two ways. The first is the intuitive dancer who does not count but rather feels the music and senses the rhythmic references in the music. However, the majority of these dancers do not keep accurate timing 100% of the time.

The second is the "educated" dancer who has taken classes and learned to count the beats to stay on time. This type of mental counting is the way the majority of dancers who have taken classes keep time. The reason for using counting is because it is easier to teach steps and dance patterns with counting before you actually do it with music. It gives students a reference, matching a count to a step, to keep time and to properly execute patterns and turns. When music is finally used, the student can then overlay the counting she's already been doing to connect with the music.

It must also be realized that there is a need to balance counting (an intellectual process) with feeling and moving to the rhythms that drive this music. Once dancers learn to count, it is difficult to shut that process off. But, you have to make a conscious effort to feel more than think.

> **The key to mastering your timing is knowing where the 1 beat is in the music at all times, and knowing where the 8 beat phrase begins and ends.**

The other aspect of mastering your timing is execution. Once you know where the beats are, now you have to perform the turns, styling and patterns of the dance within the "right" time, or in the "pocket."

To have total command of your dance timing you have to learn to "hear" the rhythmic patterns in the music and how those sounds relate to the beats (or counts) in the music. Knowing this will not only make you a better dancer but it will also give you a greater appreciation for the music, which helps to inspire your dance even more. Sometimes students who have a musical background ask: if I already know where the counts are, why do I need to try and listen for the different rhythms and instruments in the music? The answer has to do with the essence of why we dance – which is to connect our spirit to the spirit of the music and to express the heartfelt joy of that experience. It shifts your attention to the pure sound of rhythm, and not numbers. In this context, numbers do not exist. It produces a more organic intimacy with the rhythmic elements in the music which heightens your inspiration.

This chapter will give you insights and exercises that will help you to understand what is happening in the music and how it relates to your dance. This will be the foundation for mastering your timing.

The 3 levels of timing mastery

Level 1 – You can keep time. You find those dancers who have a music background fall into this category. They know where the counts are in the music. For "on 2" dancers this means knowing where the 2 beat is and that you're always on it. Also, the patterns and turns you perform are done at the "right time." Obviously, we're talking about the most basic requirement for dancing, but it does imply a certain level of mastery.

Level 2 – Keeps accurate timing while also adding improvisational steps and styling. At this level you begin to play with the timing. You can stretch and contract turns and patterns, or inflect your dance with certain body movements and positions. All with accurate timing.

Level 3 – Not only is your timing impeccable at this level, but there is a deeper connection with the music. There is a greater freedom to improvise, to style and to connect with you partner. There is a greater sense of musicality. Every dance is different depending on the music and the partner.

Most dancers fall between levels 1 and 2.

The Four Core Timing Elements

There are four core elements that a dancer has to know (or experience) in order to master his/her timing. These are:

1 – 4/4 timing
2 – tempo
3 – phrasing
4 - execution

4/4 timing

For our purposes, the only thing to know about 4/4 timing is that it means there are 4 beats in every measure of music. Counting to 4 is the most basic unit of counting in the music. As dancers this means that you will be counting to 4 or increments of 4 (to 8) to keep time in your dance. It is not necessary to understand anything else, but if you are interested, pick up a book on music theory and look under the section for meter and time signature.

When you're counting the beats – you have to make sure that they are even and of the same duration.

From a musician's point of view, an entire song is counted 1234-1234-1234 and so on to the end. As dancer's, we count to 8 because it fits in with the natural arrangement of salsa music and it also fits our full basic step structure (4 beats forward, 4 beats back).

An important point to understand about 4/4 timing is that it creates a structure, or matrix, over which the rhythmic patterns of sounds and melodies can take place - in this case, the sounds of salsa. These 4 beats per measure create a repetitive rhythm of strong and weak beats or pulses that complement the Afro-Cuban rhythms played over it.

Each beat in this 4 beat scheme has a particular relationship to the other. The 1 and 3 beats are downbeats, with a stronger emphasis, and the 2 and 4 beats are called upbeats and have a weaker accent than the 1 and 3 beats – so it sets up a pattern, or pulse, of strong-weak-strong-weak. <u>The strongest accent of the 4 beats is the 1 beat.</u> This last point is the reason that teachers and instructors use the 1 beat as the main reference point for keeping your timing. It is also the reason why 99.9% of dancers (before they take classes) will gravitate to dancing on the 1 beat. This is also the reason why the on2 basic step with the count of 123-567 was developed – using the idea that it will be easier to find the 2 beat if you step on the 1 beat first.

An advantage you have is that your ear is already used to hearing the sound patterns of 4/4 timing. It is the most popular time structure for many different forms of music, including rock, ballads, pop, and classical. What is needed now is to train the ear to hear how the rhythms of salsa integrate with 4/4 timing.

On a basic level, rhythmic patterns and melodies tend to begin at the 1 beat and tend to complete around the 4th beat, before it resolves back to the 1 beat. As we will see later, salsa music is organized in 8 beat segments. This means that the rhythmic phrase will begin around the 1 beat and end around the 8 beat. We listen to those rhythmic and melodic patterns, whether consciously or unconsciously, to hook into the music.

4/4 Timing and Syncopated Rhythms

Because salsa music is based on syncopated African derived rhythms, it is important to illustrate how 4/4 timing relates to syncopation. In the 4/4 time structure, the syncopated beats are the 2 and 4 beats. They are considered syncopated because the 2 and 4 beats are the weaker beats in the 4/4 time structure. When you accent a beat that is not usually emphasized it becomes syncopated. This is the simplest example of syncopation. But, it partly explains why the 2 beat was chosen to dance to these syncopated Afro/Cuban rhythms – because the 2 beat is considered syncopated, it allows the basic step (in a simplistic way) to align to the syncopated Afro/Cuban rhythms.

The Afro/Cuban rhythms are more complex in their syncopation, but like the 2 and 4 beat syncopations, they relate back to 4/4 timing. Remember, there are two basic pulses going on in the music. The first is the 4/4 pulse, and the second is the rhythmic pulse of the Afro/Cuban based rhythms. They are both integrated and work together.

The chart below illustrates four instruments in the rhythm section and how their syncopated rhythms relate to the beats in the music. The chart shows the count broken out to include the off beats or eighth notes. The off-beats are all the columns with the "&" symbol. In music these beats refer to eighth notes. As you notice, they fall evenly at the midpoint between each regular beat.

Counts	1	&	2	&	3	&	4	&	5	&	6	&	7	&	8	&
Clave			X		X				X			X			X	
Conga			X				X	X			X				X	X
Bass				X			X					X			X	
Cowbell	X		X	X	X		X	X	X		X	X	X		X	X

The "X" represents the main accents for 4 rhythm section instruments – clave, conga, bass, and cowbell. As you can see from the chart, the majority of the accented beats fall on syncopated beats, meaning, other than the 1 beat or 3 beat (or the 5 and 7 beats when counting to 8). This is another reason many dancers have difficulty with salsa timing.

The good new is, to develop your timing you don't have to worry about the off-beats. For social dancing we are only concerned with the beats 1, 2, 3, and 4. The syncopation and playing with the off-beats in the music comes into play later on in your development, through improvised footwork, styling, body movements and gestures.

Tempo

Tempo is how fast the music is being played. For dancers, this translates into how fast you count, and how fast you will be taking your steps. Knowing the tempo works hand-in-hand with counting the 4 beats per measure, and counting in general. Marking the tempo and counting the beats is essentially the same thing.

For example, if you are counting the beats in the measure or bar of music, it would go like this – 1234 –1234 -1234 etc. or, if you count to 8 it would go like this: 1234-5678 1234-5678 1234-5678, and so on. How <u>fast</u> you count these beats is what tempo is.

Measures	1				2				3				4			
4 Count	1	2	3	4	1	2	3	4	1	2	3	4	1	2	3	4
8 Count	1	2	3	4	5	6	7	8	1	2	3	4	5	6	7	8
Taps	/	/	/	/	/	/	/	/	/	/	/	/	/	/	/	/
Basic Step	X	X	X		X	X	X		X	X	X		X	X	X	

The above chart shows the relationship between tapping, counting the 4 beats per measure, and the basic step. The tapping row represents marking the tempo – which is tapping on every beat. When you tap, you are hitting at the same place as the 4 counts in the music. Notice also, that when you do your basic step you are marking out the tempo through your feet. This table also reveals an important aspect of maintaining good timing. This has to do with taking even steps on each beat, and making sure you account, always, to the beat you **don't** step on – in this case the 4 beat (and 8 beat if you count to 8).

Anyone who has listened to music will usually tap their foot or snap their fingers on every other beat. This is a modified way of hooking into the tempo of the music.

Whenever you listen to music, try to figure out the tempo by tapping or clapping to the music in the same way as the taps column in the chart above.

Phrasing

Phrasing refers to a rhythmic pattern that has a beginning and an end and then repeats itself. In salsa music, rhythmic patterns, or phrases, are what make up the music. It is in the rhythms (patterns) played by the rhythm section where you will be able to recognize the consistent and regular patterns for finding where the 1 beat occurs.

> **Developing the ear to hear how rhythmic patterns relate to the counting - finding the one beat – is the KEY to your timing!**

An example of a simple rhythmic phrase, or pattern, is the conga rhythm, also called *tumbao*. The conga plays two main accents: on beat 2 and beat 4. You can see immediately that the *tumbao* is playing on the two syncopated rhythms of the 4/4 time structure.

The following diagram shows the conga rhythm and how it relates to the counts and 4/4 timing.

4 Count	1	&	2	&	3	&	4	&	1	&	2	&	3	&	4	&
8 count	1	&	2	&	3	&	4	&	5	&	6	&	7	&	8	&
Conga			X				X	X			X				X	X

156

The conga phrase takes only <u>4 beats</u> to complete, before it repeats. Notice in the chart how the conga accents create a visual pattern of one X and two X's. The conga rhythm will let you know where the 2 and 4 beats are in the music, and from that you can find the 1 beat and 3 beat. This is a key factor in learning to understand timing. By familiarizing yourself with how certain rhythmic phrases align themselves with 4/4 timing, you will be training your ear to find the reference point that takes you to the 1 beat, as well as the other beats.

Note, if you are just listening to the conga drum rhythm, you do not have to count to 8, although you could. The reason for this is that the conga only takes 4 beats to complete, and then repeats, so there is no 8-beat reference.

The 8 Beat Phrase

Salsa music is written and arranged in 8 beat chunks, or phrases. This means that for salsa music the basic unit of phrasing is 8 beats, instead of the 4 beats of the 4/4 time structure. It is this 8 beat phrasing that dancers use to count their basic step and align with the music.

The 8 beat rhythmic organization of the music is the result of the rhythmic force of the clave. In other words, the clave (an 8 beat phrase) is what has shaped the structure of this music to 8 beats. Coincidently, this 8 beat structure fits in perfectly with the dancer's 8 beat basic step structure. For these reasons, we will focus predominantly on 8 beat phrasing to work out our timing. But, you should also realize that, technically, you can keep time just as well by counting to 4.

The main instruments we use to pick up this phrasing in the music are from the rhythm section. These include the conga, bongos, cowbell, timbales, piano, and bass. What these instruments all have in common is that they each play rhythmic phrases that take place over 8 beats, or in the case of the conga, complement the 8 beat phrasing. The combined effect of these rhythms will produce the "salsa sound."

The other instruments in the music, those that play above the rhythm section – brass, violins, singing, vibes, etc., are also references that guide us to where the beats are in the music. The rhythmic lines they play are also governed by the 8 beat structure. While they may not be as consistent as the rhythm section, which is always being played, their sound embellishes the structure and helps to highlight the 8-beat rhythmic structure. This means that every sound in the music will help to take you to the 8 beat phrase, and to the 1 beat.

Of all the instruments in the rhythm section, the piano line is the one that is the most accessible in hearing the 8 beat phrasing. This is because of its melodic and harmonic attributes. The melody line allows you to hear the rhythmic phrasing more distinctly. Another good, pure rhythmic pattern to help in hearing the 8 beat phrasing is the cascara rhythm played on the timbales. In fact, the piano line is very similar to the cascara rhythm. In this case, there is no melody or harmony, it is just rhythm.

Working with the cascara rhythm and piano lines will help take your timing to the next level. You should get to the point that you can keep accurate timing with just the cascara rhythm. In time, by cultivating the ability to hear key rhythmic phrases, there comes a point when you develop a general "sense" of the rhythmic phrases and how they fall into the 8 beat count. This means that without listening to anything in particular, you can hear the shape of the phrasing and where the 1 beat falls.

See appendix B for more information on a timing CD with music to practice with.

Execution

Execution has to do with performing the patterns and turns that make up a salsa dance. And, of course, to execute the lead and follow, proper timing is essential. Execution as it relates to timing is broken up into three parts. These are preparation,   carrying out the movement (a turn or pattern), and then the recovery. In reality, these steps all work together and can be looked as one continuous flow of movement. As the dance is initiated by the leader, it is the lead that begins the process of execution. Once the leader indicates a turn or pattern via the preparation, it is then up to the follower to process the signal and execute what the lead intended and then come out of it (the recovery) – back into the basic step. All of this is taking place within the timing of the basic step. During the follower's execution the leader is constantly aligning himself to prepare for what he will lead next. This alignment takes the form of hand-holds, positioning to his partner, and connection.

All of this takes into consideration how fast a movement has to take place to be able to harmonize with the timing and go back to the proper basic step position.

The ability to execute patterns comes through continuous dancing. As you progress in your abilities, and expand your repertoire of moves, and dance with better dancers, you will know when a pattern feels right. This is an ongoing process. Unfortunately, there are leaders (and followers) who are so caught up in wanting to learn cool moves that they don't work on perfecting their execution.   This results in sloppy dancing. This is ok when you're working it out and getting used to a new move, but eventually you want to get to the point where you have complete command over it.

Applying the Core Principles – Finding the 1 beat

The key to your timing is developing the "ear" to sense how the phrasing of the instruments work together and fall into the 8 beat timing structure. When you develop this sense you will always know where the 1 beat is in the music, as well as where the other beats are. Why the 1 beat? The pattern of the 8 beat structure is such that the rhythmic momentum it creates wants to bring us back, or to resolve itself back to the 1 beat. The 1 beat can be looked at as a home base for this 8 beat phrasing. Also, there is a natural tendency to want to start the counting from the first beat – or one.

Tracking the 1 beat

As was mentioned, being aware of where the 1 beat is will anchor your timing, and by extension, align all aspects of your dance. For this reason we will focus on locating the 1 beat.

There are 2 ways to track the 1 beat:
- you can track it every 4 beats
- you can track it every 8 beats

Tracking the 1 beat every 4 beats

This is not a common way to count for most dancers. But, it can work just as well. Most dancers are used to counting to 8.

One important note about counting to 4 in your dance is that you will not be aligning yourself to any scheme of going forward or back on any particular beat. For example, for on2 dancers this means that for the guy, he won't have a reference for going forward on the 6 beat, or going back on the 6 beat. For some dancers, this has become a major issue, but in reality, it doesn't make any difference. The point is that you will still be dancing "in time" with the music if you only count to 4. However, if you want to align yourself with the 8 beat phrasing, then you will have to count to 8.

Tracking the 1 beat every 8 beats

This is the counting that most dancers use. There are two reasons for this. The first is that it's a good way to teach the dance - having a specific count for each step in your forward and back basic. This means that if you count the 6 beat forward, then the back breaking step will always fall on the 2 beat, and that's the way you keep the dance from beginning to end. It's an excellent way to keep track of where in your basic step you should be while doing turn patterns or shine steps.

The second reason for counting to 8 is because the music is made up of 8 beat segments.

This second reason brings up a very important point for dancers that count to 8. To count to 8 correctly, you have to make sure that your count is in sync with the 8 beat musical phrase the music is following. In other words, you just can't start counting to 8 just because you know where the 1 beat is. You have to make sure that <u>it is the 1 beat that starts the 8 beat phrase</u> in the music.

Knowing where the 8 beat phrase begins in the music can be a problem for many dancers. The challenge is not only finding the 1 beat, but, finding the 1 beat in relationship to the 8 beat musical phrase. Some people refer to this as counting with the clave. Note, while the clave is "always" involved with the music (directly or indirectly), it is not necessary

162

to know anything about the clave to learn where this 8 beat phrase happens. Usually, when dancers mention the clave, it has more to do with trying to sound like they're saying something "deep" than with anything that really makes practical sense. Because most dancers do not know what part the clave really plays in the music and the dance, it creates confusion and vagueness in their understanding of the dance. See the clave section for more information.

The problem of starting the 8 beat count at the wrong point in the music is illustrated in the table below.

Row	Measures of Music	1	2	3	4
1	4 Count	1 2 3 4	1 2 3 4	1 2 3 4	1 2 3 4
2	8 beat phrase in music	1 2 3 4	5 6 7 8	1 2 3 4	5 6 7 8`
3	8 Count in Sync with Music	1 2 3 4	5 6 7 8	1 2 3 4	5 6 7 8
4	8 Count Out of Sync with Music		1 2 3 4	5 6 7 8	1 2 3 4

When a dancer counts correctly (row 3), he is in sync with the natural phrasing of the music (row 2).

The mistake dancers make with the 8 count is shown in the 4th row. Notice that the dancer begins counting 1 at the count of 5 in the music phrase. His counting is not reflecting the count of the music correctly.

The question now has to be asked – will counting out of sync with the music throw your dance off? The answer is yes and no! You will still be able to dance without any problems. Why? It is because when you start the count of 1 on the 5 beat of the phrasing, you are still aligned properly with the music and the basic step. In other words, the 5 beat is still really the 1 beat; the 6 beat is still really the 2 beat, and so on. When you count incorrectly (row 4), you are still aligned with the beats in relationship to your basic step. The worst thing that has happened is that you have mislabeled the counts - calling the 1 beat 5 and the 2 beat 6, but the 5 beat is the 1 beat and the 6 beat is the 2 beat – when you count to four. Of course, it also means that your basic step direction is out of alignment with the count. This is the "yes" part of the answer – which is a mental misalignment. Instead of going forward on 6, you're actually going back on 6.

Even though you can dance by counting the 8 beats out of sync with the musical 8 beats, you should continue to learn the phrasing in the music so you can count it properly.

After a while you should be able to pick out where the counts are by hearing just one melodic instrument, such as a piano, bass, trumpet, violin, etc. Of course, the instrument has to be playing a consistent rhythmic phrase.

Lets isolate some key rhythm section instruments and the rhythmic phrasing each one plays. We can then see how each of these phrasings relate to the 4/4 time structure, and the 8 beat phrasing, which will take us to the 1 beat. Be aware that while I am trying to explain these rhythmic sounds through words, there is no substitution for hearing the actual instruments. For this I suggest that you use my timing CD – see appendix B for more information.

It's interesting to note that in keeping with the African model of rhythm, all these sounds have a call-and –response quality to them. In fact, our basic step has this same quality.
Remember, the rhythmic phrasing will let us know two things: the tempo, and a reference for finding the 1 beat.

Conga

The conga rhythm is the most consistent sound of the rhythm section. It would be extremely beneficial to familiarize yourself with the conga rhythm (also known as *tumbao*). It not only helps to connect you more into the music, but is an important reference for maintaining your timing.

The conga rhythm has two main accents. These accents fall on the 2 beat and the 4 beat. The 2 beat is where the dry sounding slap occurs, and the 4 beat is where the two open sounds occur. There are usually two open sounds that are played over the 4 beat. These two open accents sound something like "toom-toom". The slap sound is higher pitched and sounds something like a quick "pah" sound, or it can sound at times like a high-pitched wooden block.

The two main sounds of the conga enable us to locate the 2 beat and the 4 beat. From this we can find the in-between beats of 1 and 2. In time, you should be able to know the conga rhythm sound so well that you can pick out where the conga should be playing in every song you hear, even if you don't hear it. It's almost as if you are the conga player.

Finding the 1 beat using the conga rhythm

The open sounds on the 4 beat are the key to getting to the 1 beat using the conga rhythm. Naturally, the 1 beat comes after the 4 beat.
We can vocalize the counts and the conga sound like this:
 toom-tomm 1-2-3 toom-toom 1-2-3 toom-toom 1-2-3...and so on.
The tuum-tuum sound being the counts "4 and". Remember, the 2 beat is always the slap or "plah" sound.

Piano Line

The piano is used more as a rhythmic instrument as opposed to a melodic or harmonic one. This is the reason we can use it as a reference for our timing. The piano is technically a percussion instrument.

Depending on the arrangement, the piano line is usually very consistent, especially during the swinging part of the song. If you don't know what the swinging part of the song is then see appendix C. In some arrangements, during the beginning of the song, the piano may be used more for filling and accenting without playing at all times.

It is when the piano line is a consistent rhythmic phrase, what is called a *montuno*, or *guajeo* (these are repeating vamps), that we can use it to hook into our timing with accuracy.

The thing to notice about the piano line is how its phrasing has a beginning and an end. Although it is very rhythmic, there is an emphasis in the melody and rhythm that you can use to tell where the beginning of the phrase is, so that you know when it repeats. Usually this piano line extends over 8 beats, or 2 bars – the same as clave, and the same as your basic step. The beginning of this piano phrase tends to fall on or around the 1 beat.

Cowbell

The cowbell is not usually played during the entire song. For example, it is not played during a piano solo, or during the singer's introductory verses. It is only when the chorus comes in, or the music picks up, that the typical cowbell pattern is played. There are also songs that maintain a cowbell pattern throughout from beginning to end. It depends on the musical arrangement.

The cowbell pattern is very much like a conga rhythm played double-time. If you were to mimic the typical cowbell pattern it would go like this:

```
X   X X   X   X X   X   X X   X   X X   X
1   2 &   3   4 & 1   2 &   3   4 & 1
Toom Ti-ki toom  ti-ki toom  ti-ki toom  ti-ki toom...and repeats
```

You can see this similar rhythmic pattern of 1 against 2 in the rhythm the conga plays. The conga plays the slap sound on the 2 beat, and the two open sounds are played on the 4 beat. For the cowbell this pattern is doubled. It plays the one open sound on the 1 beat, the double high-pitched sound on the 2 beat, the one open sound on the 3 beat, and the double high-pitched sounds on the 4 beat. You can begin to see how the various rhythmic elements piggyback the same pattern on each other. The effect of this is to drive the music and make it more danceable.

Finding the 1 beat with the cowbell

The open sound of the cowbell is played always on the 1 beat and the 3 beat. These are key reference points. When we listen to the cowbell with the other rhythm instruments, it provides another key to guiding us to the 1 beat. For example, when listening to the conga drum, along with the cowbell, we can use the "toom-toom" of the conga, which is always on the 4 beat, to then hear right after that the "toom" sound of the cowbell, which will be marking the 1 beat.

4 Count	1	&	2	&	3	&	4	&	1	&	2	&	3	&	4	&
8 Count	1	&	2	&	3	&	4	&	5	&	6	&	7	&	8	&
Cowbell	X		X	X	X		X	X	X		X	X	X		X	X

The above table shows the counts with the cowbell accents. Remember, the 1, 3, 5 and 7 beats get open sounds (the toom sound) and the high-pitched sound (the tiki sound) are on 2&, 4&, 6&, and 8&.

Another important point about the cowbell is that it marks time and tempo. It does this because it plays on every beat.   Listening to the cowbell helps in keeping your timing to the beats, and in hearing where certain beats fall.

Note, the cowbell does play an 8 beat phrase. It depends on the arrangement of the music. In the above example, the cowbell is playing the same rhythmic pattern every 4 beats – so there is no change from one measure to another.

If we use the 8 beat phrase version it will look like the following table.

	1	&	2	&	3	&	4	&	1	&	2	&	3	&	4	&
4 Count	1	&	2	&	3	&	4	&	1	&	2	&	3	&	4	&
8 Count	1	&	2	&	3	&	4	&	5	&	6	&	7	&	8	&
Cowbell	X		X		X		X	X	X		X	X	X		X	X
Clave			X		X				X			X		X		

Notice that the shaded box in the cowbell row (between the 2 and 3 beats) does not have an "X". This is because the cowbell, in playing an 8 beat pattern, will play exactly with the clave (see clave row) beats for beats 2 and 3. In this way, by dropping out one accent over 8 beats, it creates an 8 beat phrase pattern.

A great exercise is to dance with the cowbell, playing the 8 beat pattern version. Because it is an 8 beat phrase, you can count to eight and dance your basic step to it. This also means that you will be able to find the 1 beat to start on. The challenge is, if you're dancing on2, is to establish the dance and maintain accurate timing throughout. The rewards for working it this way will be great. As in dancing to just the conga drum, after a while you could drop the counting altogether. You will be integrated and playing off the cowbell, or having a call and response type experience.

Bass Line

The bass line also follows a similar pattern as the piano. In the beginning of the arrangement it may not play a consistent pattern. Rather, it fills in according to the arrangement, going back and forth between hitting breaks and driving the music. However, when the music gets "swinging" it will usually play a specific rhythmic and melodic phrase that revolves around two "key" notes per measure of music.

The two key notes of the "swinging" bass line fall on the "and of 2", meaning the midpoint between the 2nd and 3rd beats (or the 6 and 7 beat when counting to 8), and the other beat falls on the 4 beat.

An interesting point about the bass line is that for many dancers, before they take classes, they will hook into the bass line and end up dancing on the 3 beat. This is because one of the main accents of the bass is played on the "and" of the 2 beat. The "and" of the 2 beat means that the bass note is played at the exact midpoint between the 2 beat and the 3 beat. In musical terms we would call this an eighth note. Because the "and" of 2 falls very close to the 3 beat, this "and" beat becomes a reference point for these dancers, which leads them to dance on the 3 beat.

Summary

As you work more and more with familiarizing yourself with these rhythmic patterns, you will develop the sense and the awareness of the rhythmic "shape" of the music. As you hear the entire sound of a song you will know exactly where the 1 beat is and where the 8 beat phrase begins and ends.

Also, in the beginning you can practice by working with one instrument. Make sure that you can dance to that instrument with 100% accuracy. Then, move on to another instrument. After you have those two working well, listen to them together, and dance to it. When you get to this point, you will experience the interplay between the two sounds. If you work with this enough, you will begin to hear both sounds as one sound. The interplay will merge into a flowing sound where your listening and your steps become completely integrated.

Counting to 8

You have already been introduced to how the 8 counts relate to the music, and of course, to your basic step. Let's look at a few more points in dealing with counting to 8.

There are 2 ways of counting.

1 - Musicians counting - This is counting only to 4 – following the music straight

A musician would count like this:

1-2-3-4 1-2-3-4 1-2-3-4 1-2-3-4 1-2-3-4... and so on

2 - Dancers counting - This is counting up to 8.

A dancer would count like this

1-2-3-5-6-7 1-2-3-5-6-7 1-2-3-5-6-7   1-2-3-5-6-7...etc. the reason they leave out the 4 and 8 is because these are the two hold beats in the basic.

A note on instructor counting: there are some instructors who count their basic step consecutively, meaning they count their forward basic as 123, and their back basic as 456. They do not include the hold, or pause step, in the basic step count. While people can learn it this way it is not conducive for connecting with the music. It's more beneficial for the dancer to count with the music than to artificially count just the basic steps. The other point is that by including the hold count you will be aware of the pause step in your dance. One of the problems beginners have is making sure they account for that pause step.

The following count table will help you to understand the relationship between these 2 counts.

Musicians	1-2-3-4	1-2-3-4	1-2-3-4	1-2-3-4
8 Beat Phrase	1-2-3-4	5-6-7-8	1-2-3-4	5-6-7-8
Dancers Count	1-2-3-4	5-6-7-8	1-2-3-4	5-6-7-8

Why we count up to 8

All counting is for instructional purposes only. It's a straightforward way to associate a specific count (or number) to a specific step (within the basic step). Because all initial instruction is done without music, counting to set a tempo and set your basic step is the perfect way to practice before doing it with the music. The reason it goes up to eight is because your complete basic step (forward and back) takes up 8 beats of music, or 2 bars of music. Your forward basic (3 steps and a pause) is done over 4 beats. Your back basic (3 steps and a pause) is done over 4 beats. Add them both up and you get 8.

The other reason for counting to 8 is to distinguish between your forward basic and back basic. In this way, when we are learning a complicated step or pattern we will know where in our basic step we should be at all times.

Keep in mind, even though we count to 8, the counts of 5-6-7-8 are the same as the counts 1-2-3-4 in the music. The count 5 is still the 1 beat, the count 6 is still the 2 beat, the count 7 is still the 3 beat, and the count 8 is still the 4 beat. We increment to 8 in order to give each step in the basic a unique identifier.

Forward on 6 and Back on 2?

What has become something of a standard in dance classes and social dancing is that men will go forward on the 6 count, and go back on the 2 beat. It is the opposite for women – they go forward on 2 and back on the count of 6. The 6 forward has become known as men's timing, and the 2 forward has become known as ladies timing.

While this is what everyone teaches it must be pointed out that this is totally arbitrary. At some point someone made a choice that men go forward on 6 and ladies back on 6. And the next generation of instructors followed this scheme blindly. So let's ask the basic question – why? No one can give any real reason for it. The most they can come up with is a contrived chivalrous explanation of allowing the women to come forward when they start – which is not really a valid reason. There is absolutely nothing un-chivalrous about starting forward.

The point to this is that there is no "real" reason for the man to go forward on the 6 count, and the lady to go back on the 6 count. It does not matter. There is nothing inherent in the music or the basic step that demands that the man go forward during the 6 beat of the 8 beat musical phrase. Some say, well, it feels right. The answer to this is, of course it feels right because that's all you've been doing. It comes down to the force of blind habit. It was a choice some dancer made and that's all. Over time, when enough people do something a certain way and it becomes accepted to the point of gospel, does the perception that this is the "only" way to do it becomes set. The point is to be aware that it is only a choice, and dancing with the man going forward on 2 is just as valid.

Common reasons why dancers get off their timing

The Basic step is weak.

This is the number one reason dancers lose their timing. The first and most important condition for having good timing is to have a strong basic step. This means that in executing turns and patterns, your basic step is exactly where it should be. This is why working with the basic step is the most important element that every dancer needs to do to improve. This means working slowly to make sure that basic steps and turns are being done exactly the way it should.

It is especially important to make sure you account for the pause step. The pause step could also be a traveling step where the foot is in the air preparing to step on the next beat. The pause step requires that you account for one beat before stepping with your next basic step. Many beginners have a tendency to rush this step, especially after a turn and end up with their steps thrown off.

Losing Tempo through your Basic Step

This goes hand-in-hand with having a weak basic step. You have to know the speed of the music – how fast the beats are going – in order to take your basic steps properly. One of the biggest mistakes beginners make is speeding up, especially if the song is slow. This requires really listening to the music, and working with the phrasing so that you know exactly how fast the beats are being played, and that your steps are taken at the same speed as the musical beats

Many dancers want to just get out and do it. This is great, but what happens is that in the process of having fun and expressing themselves, the timing suffers. If your timing is shaky to begin with, you have to give yourself some time to really work with the music. It takes time and focus, but you can do it - and if you want to be a good, or great dancer, than you have to master the timing. I produced an excellent Timing CD (see appendix B for more information) that will help you in developing the hearing skills to master your timing.

Appendix A

The Son

The *son* (pronounced soh-ng in Spanish) was a rhythmic revolution in Cuba. Dancers fell in love with its swinging earthy sounds. Its influence was so strong that the charanga groups adapted it to the *danzon*. In *son* we see the first clear path that will take us straight to what will be come known as mambo. *Son* incorporated vocals, percussion, and string instruments.

A main characteristic of the *son* was the use of the *tres*. The *tres* is a three-stringed guitar that has each of its strings doubled. It is through the use and development of the *tres* that a swinging rhythmic and melodic sound is introduced. This rhythmic drive would be called *montuno*, or *guajeo*. A *montuno* is simply a vamp that repeats over two to four measures of music – in the same way as a piano line. When you hear a driving piano vamp in a salsa song, its origins can be traced back to the *tres* in the early 1900's.

The basic rhythm section of a *son* group was the use of the bongos, maracas, clave, and bass. The bongos took on a greater role as accompanist, and the clave became a rhythmic conductor that shaped and held the sounds together.

The *son* developed in the province of Oriente, which is in the eastern part of rural Cuba. It is here where a greater integration of blacks and whites allowed for a beautiful blend of African and European influences.

It is said that the origins of the *son* go back to the 16th century, and was influenced by blacks from Haiti who developed the sound that was to change the course of Cuban music and dance. Also, related to the development of the son were the *Changui* and the *Nengon*. Both of these styles came before the *son*. However, they shared the use of the *tres* as the main melodic instrument, with simpler percussion instruments to accompany it. These percussion instruments included the *marimbula* (a type of hand piano), *botija* (a jar with a hole in one side), bongo and scraper.

By the early 1900's, the *son* had spread throughout much of Cuba. It reached Havana in 1920. An interesting historical note of the *son* was that it was banned and outlawed by the Cuban government because of the riots and controversy it would generate. When the *son* was played there would be a "sonero" (singer) who would sing lyrics that contained protests of slavery, double meanings that would contain insults, clever in-directives that would question manhood, fidelity, or a woman's faithfulness. These *sones* would be played at parties and festivals, and the best *soneros* would get together and try to outdo the other. However, it would sometimes get to the point that an insult was intolerable and fighting would breakout.

At times the army would be brought in to bring order to these areas where they played *son*. In fact, one of the reasons given for the migration of the *son* to the city of Havana was that soldiers who were also musicians, came back from the rural areas and began playing and spreading what they heard. What also helped spread the *son* was the migration of rural workers to the big cities.

The son also went by the name *son montuno*. *Montuno* refers to the mountains. This is in reference to the fact that son developed in the rural, mountain areas of Cuba.

An important effect of the son was that the higher social classes were attracted to it. The *son*, in merging musical elements of African and European cultures in a harmonious way, became the dominant music form in Cuba. Although it was considered by many to be low-class music, its infectious rhythms won the hearts of the Cuban people of all social classes.

One of the main reasons for its popularity was the recordings of the Sexteto Habanero. The sextet consisted of clave, bongos, maracas, bass, tres, and guitar. By 1925, many of their recordings became best sellers. One of their most famous recordings is *Tres Lindas Cubanas*, which has become a favorite of Cubans to this day. That same year they won a competition for the best *son* orchestra. In 1927, the group became a septet by including a trumpet. Soon, all the *son* groups were adding a trumpet.

Another group that had a great influence on the son movement was the Septeto Nacional, led by Ignacio Piñeiro. Piñeiro was a great innovator and composer of the *son*. He helped to establish another chapter in the development of the *son* by broadening the repertoire, as well as modifying its structure. He incorporated lyrics from various musical genres, including *rumba* and *guajiras*. He also was one of the first to begin the trend of combining these dance rhythms to produce what would be called *guajira-son*, *rumba-son*, *son-pregon*, and *guaracha-son*. Piñeiro's Septeto Nacional would surpass the Septeto Habanero in popularity. Some of his most popular tunes include *Echale Salsita*,and *Suavecito*. The song *Echale Salsita* is the first recording that makes reference to "salsa" as a means of describing this Afro-Cuban music.

Dancing to the Son

The steps that were being done with the son were similar to the *danzon*. There was a quick-quick-slow pattern through the feet where the breaking step (the main step forward and back in your basic step) begins the basic step. The dance was toned down with few turns and patterns. Of course, there were always dancers that would push the dance and incorporate fancy turns and steps. This is the way that the dance evolves.

The Contribution of Son to the modern mambo/salsa band

The following are key elements in son that would set the stage for a mambo sound.

The Anticipated Bass

This is where the bass anticipates the one beat, along with the change of harmony. This shifts the stress to the 4th beat or upbeat in the music.
Making the bass line a part of the percussive ensemble, and shifting the accent on the 4th beat is what further empowered the swing of the music. Note, the placement of this accent of the bass is driven by the clave. The accent on the 4th beat is also another African trait.

Montuno Section

The vamp of the *tres*, where two or more measures are continually repeated, creating a melodic and harmonic rhythmic swing, was a major development in the rhythmic swing of *son*. This rhythmic energy of the *tres*, later transferred to the piano, continued the invigoration of the total rhythmic swing of the music.

Vocals - Call-and-Response

Between the lead singer and the chorus (also known as coro) - another African trait that sets the structure for what would become salsa.

The innovations of the son set the stage for the next stage in the journey to mambo: *conjuntos*.

The Influence of Son in the United States

In May of 1930, a Cuban group called the Havana Casino Orchestra, led by Don Azpiazu, recorded the tune "El Manicero" (the peanut vendor) for RCA Victor. That same year, Aspiazo came to New York for an engagement at New York's Palace Theatre. During the show a dance team showcased *rumba* dancing - which was a combination of a diluted form of folkloric *rumba*, and son. Azpiazu had brought this dance group with him from Cuba. The third number they played was "El Manicero.," RCA waited 7 months before releasing their recording because they weren't sure how the American people would respond.

By 1931 it had become a national hit. "El Manicero" was a Cuban *son* taken from a musical form known as Havana *pregon* style.

The success of this tune sparked the *rumba* craze in the United States. For the first time Americans heard an authentic Cuban sound. Before this Americans were used to watered-down versions of Latin songs and rhythms. It was more rhythmic than what they were used to, which was reflected in the descriptions of the music as savage, wild, and exotic.

With "El Manicero" Cuban *son*, and Latin music in general, established themselves as an integral part of the American music and dance scene. It was a pivotal time that established in the American ear an appreciation for Cuban music. You can say that the *rumba* craze primed America for the next Latin explosion that would come in twenty years – mambo.

Appendix B

Mastering Salsa/Mambo Timing CD and Ebook

This CD is your essential guide to understanding salsa rhythms and how it relates to your dance. We don't just count over the music. We teach you what the 3 Core Principles are and why they're necessary for mastering your timing!

Train your ear to "hear" where the beats are in the music with our innovative exercises.

Test your progress with practice dance tracks featuring fade-in, fade-out counts, unique "basic step guide" and "on 2 guide".

This CD is designed for ALL salseros, club or ballroom style, 'on1' or 'on 2'.

CD Highlights:

-Tempo Defined
-Learning How to Listen & Count
-Phrasing - The Real "Key"
-Rhythm Review: Conga & Tumbao, Clave, Cowbell, Piano, Bass & Cascara
-26 Instructional & Practice Tracks
-4 Bonus Dance Tracks with "On 2 Guide"

Mastering Salsa/Mambo Timing – The Practice CD

This supplement to our Instructional Timing CD will make sure that when you practice (full length music), you will never lose your timing.

With over 60 minutes of music, you will have many tracks to practice with to hone your timing skills.

With Fade-in/Fade out counting and with our unique Basic Step Guide you will develop your ear to always find the 8 beat phrasing, and make sure your basic step is clean and precise.

CD Highlights

-Over 60 Minutes of Great Music
-Slow and Fast Conga Tracks
-11 Rhythm Section Tracks - Including 7 Piano Line Tracks
-Full Songs with Counting and Basic Step Guide as well as with Music Only
-Cha Cha Included
-Email Document Explaining All Tracks

To order please go to www.thesalsaexpert.com

Appendix C

Anatomy of a Salsa Song

A salsa song will usually consist of 4 main parts:
1- Introduction and verse
2- Montuno
3- Mambo
4- Montuno

1 – Introduction and verse

This is the beginning of the song. The band will usually play an instrumental opening, which leads to the lead singer singing various verses.

2 – Montuno

This is the part in the music when the intensity of the music picks up, making it more "danceable." The rhythm section picks up momentum by creating a greater drive: the coro (chorus) comes in, the lead singer will improvise tasty rhythmic lines in a call and response fashion with the coro, the piano plays a repeated vamp (called montuno), the cowbell comes in, the bass line becomes more rhythmic. All these factors will push the rhythmic intensity to a higher level. This is the "swinging" part of the salsa song.

3 – Mambo

This section is a kind of bridge section that is usually instrumental. The horn lines will introduce new melodic and harmonic patterns. The piano and bass will also change their rhythmic emphasis, in order to create a contrast with the *montuno* section sound.

4 – Montuno

This is a return to the coro/lead singer interplay and main "swing" part of the song. Solos can also be taken during this section.

A general note about these 4 parts is that each section is usually separated by what is called *cierres*. *Cierres* are breaks in the music where the band will play "break" figures together to lead into the next section.